A JOURNEY THROUGH
NEW ZEALAND FILM

IAN BRODIE

HarperCollins*Publishers*

The author and publishers wish to thank Investment New Zealand
and Tourism New Zealand for their assistance in producing this book.

National Library of New Zealand Cataloguing-in-Publication Data
    Brodie, Ian, 1957-
    A journey through New Zealand film / Ian Brodie.
    Includes index.
    ISBN-10: 1-86950-610-3
    1. Motion picture locations—New Zealand—Guidebooks. 2. New
    Zealand—Guidebooks. I. Title.
    791.430250993—dc 22

First published 2006
HarperCollins*Publishers (NewZealand) Limited*
P.O. Box 1, Auckland

Photograph page 9 by Geoff Short, photographs pages 34 and 35 by John Toon, photograph
bottom left page 134 courtesy Chris Hinch. All other photographs by Ian Brodie.

Ian Brodie asserts the moral right to be identified as the author of this work.

ISBN 186950 610 3

Cover design by Katy Wright, HarperCollins Design Studio
Typesetting by IslandBridge

Printed in China, on 128gsm matt

Previous: The calm waters of Glendhu Bay.
Centre right is the hill the Fellowship
walked around in *The Fellowship of the
Ring*, whilst the 3033 m high Mt Aspiring in
the background appeared in the opening
sequence of *The Two Towers*.

This book has been a journey for me in so many ways. A reaffirmation of my love of New Zealand film, visits to wonderful locations and, most importantly, the fantastic people who have helped my quest. In an effort to thank everybody I am sure I will omit someone — please be assured this is not intentional.

Charles Eggen — a fellow lover of New Zealand film — thanks so much for all the information you have freely given me. Your website is a veritable treasure trove. Paul Voigt and Susan McFetridge from Investment NZ and Jane Dent, Joanna Cheok and Gina Williams from Tourism NZ have all helped make this book possible.

Don Stafford helped so much with my understanding of Maoridom, and finding my way around New Zealand has been so easy with the help of maps from John McCombs at Map Toaster Topo. Some special thanks are owed to Phil Makanna for introducing me to the Apple Mac G5, Kens Imaging in Christchurch for photographic support, Don Sharpe at Imagelab for easing my nerves and Chris Hinch for listening.

I met some great people on the road — Katherine Novak, Sue Radcliffe and Niko Tangaroa especially.

On Film magazine has been a wonderful resource — thanks to the editor, Nick Grant.

Thanks to the contributors — Tim Sanders, Gaylene Preston, John Toon and Russell Alexander — and to Roger Donaldson for a superb foreword.

Once again I have two families to thank. My editor Lorain Day deserves so many thanks and hugs; along with Tony Fisk and Lorraine Steele, you are a wonderful team.

Last — and most especially — to my wife, Dianne, and children, Travis and Sally-Anne — thanks for everything.

Ian Brodie

Acknowledgements

Foreword

The art of successful filmmaking in New Zealand relies upon many things. Great scripts, gifted directors and producers, talented actors, dedicated, professional crews and our truly spectacular and varied locations.

Many years ago, on one of my first trips to the USA, I remember people asking me where I was from. When I said New Zealand, they asked two questions… *Do they speak English there* and *Where is it?* Those days are long gone and we have our movies to thank for that.

The films represented in this book have literally put New Zealand on the map. They are a testament to the clever, hard-working and ambitious Kiwis involved.

The filmmakers set out on each project with no guarantee of success. Only their optimism, enthusiasm and utter determination, as well as their passion for the art of film, made these movies a reality.

Filmmaking is a collaborative enterprise and maybe this is why so many successful films have come out of our tiny country. We have loved seeing ourselves on film. If you look at a list of the biggest grossing films in New Zealand history, half the spots in the top twenty, are taken by local productions.

Everyone understands film production makes an enormous contribution to the cultural and economic wellbeing of the nation. From the top down, the whole country really gets behind the idea that we can take on the world with our homegrown expertise and passion. Everyone knows someone who has worked on a New Zealand movie.

Many of our films have become an integral part of New Zealand culture, especially so for the residents of those places where these movies have been shot. Film crews rolled into 'small town' New Zealand and transformed the familiar into something unreal and exciting.

Many a school kid has ducked classes and waited patiently to catch a glimpse of the action, whether it was a yellow Mini smashing through a shop window in Queenstown or the back of Tom Cruise's head as he stepped onto a plane in New Plymouth.

Peter Jackson's *The Lord of the Rings Trilogy*, and Andrew Adamson's *The Chronicles of Narnia: The Lion, the Witch and the Wardrobe* are the latest movies to take New Zealand filmmaking to new heights. These films have had a huge impact on the lives of thousands of New Zealanders and have become legends in the rest of the world.

New Zealand films have always made good use of the landscape and now the whole world is coming to know just how amazing our country really is. Where else in the world, in a country the size of California, does such diverse and outstanding scenery exist?

Hundreds of kilometres of accessible untouched beaches, thousands of hectares of mountains and bush; from the top of the North Island to the bottom of the South Island it is such a dramatic and magnificent land.

This book guides the traveller through those places, and celebrates a filmmaking history we Kiwis should be proud of.

Roger Donaldson

Roger Donaldson

The land

*Te whenua he whaea
e kore e mate.*

*The land is a mother
that never dies.*

This Maori whakatauaki (proverb) sums up an attitude many Maori and Pakeha hold for the land. It is deeply embedded in our culture in a general sense and infuses New Zealand filmmaking with a spirit that permeates through the drama.

I grew up in two very different landscapes. My first ten years or more were spent living under the black foothills of the Southern Alps on the West Coast of the South Island — a thin coastal strip of dramatic treacherous beauty fringed by a pounding sea that rattles boulders and occasionally hurls coastal ships at the dangerous river shingle bars.

Then we moved to 'Sunny Napier' in Hawke's Bay. Benign turquoise-blue skies, and soft pink and mauves in the sunsets; the sea warm and lippy-lappy where we swam at Westshore. The Heretaunga Plains were parched in the long summers adding a bleached softness to the foothills. Not many old wooden Victorian villas in Napier. The town effervesces California — bungalows, art deco concrete colourful civic buildings and no power lines scalloping through the air above the CBD. But this open-plan city, with its Marine Parade echoing the Croisette at Cannes, has a disturbing history.

At 10.45 a.m. on 3 February 1931 it was shaken by a lethal earthquake measuring 7.8 on the Richter scale. Over 1% of the population were killed, largely because of the voracious fire that followed. The town was engulfed within an hour of the quake and reduced to Dresden-scale devastation. So that's how it is here; the place itself has a strong personality. The whole of New Zealand is a recent geological upthrust — and there's usually a terrific untold story under the sunny surface. 'It's so young it's really scary,' was the opinion of two visiting Australian filmmakers who suggested that the spooky fluidity in our storytelling was better understood once you experienced the landscape.

There's a 'vibe'. You can feel it. Often dark, sometimes simple; I have never felt it anywhere else. It flows from the secrets the land holds. Tribal histories passed on by oral storytelling to the selected few; European settlers, recent arrivals without the language to express this place. Maori mythology as enduring as Homer is overlaid here with Celtic and European storytelling. This heritage produces in our filmmaking an interesting mix. Fantasy tinged with feet-on-the-ground realism. This expressive myth-making flows from the strength, the blood, the fire and the life of the land itself. Fresh ground for a new local artform.

All up we've probably made less New Zealand films in total than are made in half a year of Hollywood production. This makes the local audience critical. They have trouble accepting our hero can run round a corner in the centre of town and arrive at somewhere else entirely. They can't abide cheats. As filmmaking is almost all cheating, this can cause uncomfortable moments for filmmakers.

Once I was with Sonja Davies, the pioneer peace campaigner, in Nelson. The audience had just watched **Bread & Roses**, the film I had directed based on her autobiography. Some of them had been present during some of the real events represented. Sonja and I weren't at all sure how they would take it. They were stunned. Dazed. Grateful. Inspired even, but there was a woman who waited until everyone had gone from the theatre then she shyly approached and asked me where we filmed a particular beach scene. I told her. 'Yes, I thought so,' she said. 'I knew that wasn't Tahunanui Beach. The sky was the wrong blue.'

Here the ground moves, mountains spit fire, the sea pounds on the long shore and the filmmakers graze, making an already beautiful landscape articulate.

Gaylene Preston

Gaylene Preston

Overleaf: Mt Taranaki (Egmont) — the Taranaki stand-in for Mt Fuji in **The Last Samurai**.

9

Contents

South Island locations   78

Introduction

This book is a celebration of films made in New Zealand and the magnificent landscapes they feature. We have a rich film heritage, which in recent years has received many accolades, and the reader will recognise these motion pictures immediately. There are others, however, not so well known in the international circuit, that are equally deserving of these tributes. If this book inspires you to watch and enjoy these films, one of my aims has been achieved.

My other objective is to showcase the many and varied landscapes that have appeared in these wonderful movies and (in many cases) been one of the major stars.

Many of the locations are 'off the beaten track' of the mainstream tourist but this does not diminish their beauty, and introducing them to our visitors will show this country is still rich in undiscovered treasures.

What the book is *not* is a complete guide to New Zealand or New Zealand films, for which I recommend one of the many comprehensive guides available and a good map.

Following this introduction are brief synopses of the films that have been included, along with cast and crew credits. I would have dearly loved to include all New Zealand films but this has not been practicable. The choice was purely mine and, if I have offended anyone by omitting a film they consider a classic, I apologise.

Following the film synopses we commence our journey through the country. We start at the top of the North Island, travel to Wellington and then return to Auckland for a flight to the South Island. The journey here is semi-geographical, as films permitted.

New Zealand filmmakers have been very supportive of this project and have included comments where practicable on their film(s). Not all had the time to complete this task, so any absences are not indicative of their unwillingness to help.

The end pages include a simplified listing of New Zealand films released at the time of writing, followed by a 'Reel of Honour' celebrating the successes we have achieved internationally.

May this book introduce you to our breathtaking combination of film and country, an amalgamation I believe has not been achieved so magically anywhere else in the world.

Ian Brodie
Wanaka, 2006

In My Father's Den

Cast: Matthew Macfadyen, Miranda Otto, Emily Barclay, Colin Moy, Vicky Haughton, Jodie Rimmer, Jimmy Keen.

Crew: Director of Photography: Stuart Dryburgh; Music: Simon Boswell; Editing: Chris Plummer; Costume Designer: Kirsty Cameron; Production Designer: Jennifer Kernke; Screenplay: Brad McGann, based on the book by Maurice Gee.

Producers: Trevor Haysom, Dixie Linder.

Director: Brad McGann.

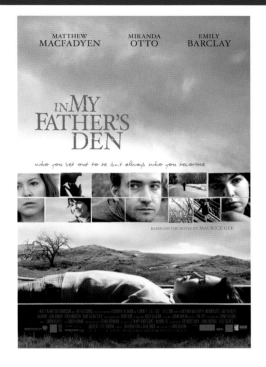

When his father dies, Paul Prior (Macfadyen), a disillusioned war photographer, returns home. His brother (Moy) pressures him into staying to help sell their father's property, where Paul rediscovers an old den. His father secretly harboured a love of wine, literature and philosophy, and Paul finds sixteen-year-old Celia (Barclay) has been using the den as a private haven.

When he takes a temporary position at the local high school, Celia is one of his students and it isn't long before their friendship comes under scrutiny. When Celia goes missing Paul faces mounting suspicions and violent threats, and as the painful truth emerges Paul is forced to confront family tragedy and betrayal.

Fifty Ways of Saying Fabulous

Set in the summer of 1975, *Fifty Ways of Saying Fabulous* is the beguiling story of 12-year-old Billy, who is about to discover that growing up is a lot more confusing than he could ever have imagined. The only son of a farmer, he is out of step with the other boys at school. They only seem to want to fight and play rugby; he tries to be the same, but knows he is not cut out to be a farmer or a rugby player. Instead he would rather dream about an imaginary life in outer space. In this world, a turnip paddock becomes a lunar landscape and a cow's tail a head of beautiful blonde hair which transforms him into Lana, the heroine of his favourite TV show.

Cast: Andrew Patterson, Harriet Beattie, Jay Collins, Michael Dorman, Georgia McNeil, Ross McKellar, Stephanie McKellar-Smith, Rima te Wiata, George Mason, Michelle O'Brien.

Crew: Editor: Peter Roberts; Photography: Simon Raby; Composer: Peter Scholes; Sound: Dick Reade; Production Designer: Ken Turner; Costume Designer: Kirsty Cameron; Make-up / Hair Design: Tracey Sharman.

Producer: Michele Fanti.

Writer and Director: Stewart Main, based on the book by Graeme Aitken.

Sleeping Dogs

Cast: Sam Neill, Ian Mune, Warren Oates, Nevan Rowe, Donna Akersten, Ian Watkin, Bill Johnson, Clyde Scott.

Crew: Screenplay: Ian Mune, Arthur Baysting (based on the C. K. Stead novel, *Smith's Dream*); Photography: Michael Seresin; Editor: Ian John; Music: Murray Grindley, David Calder, Mathew Brown.

Producer and Director: Roger Donaldson.

Against a background of economic crisis and industrial turmoil where a repressive government decides to rule by force, an apolitical man (Neill) leaves a broken marriage to set up home on an offshore island. He is completely unaware that revolutionaries are using it to store arms, but soon finds out when the police come for him. Meanwhile his wife's lover (Mune), likewise apolitical until he is unwittingly caught up in police violence at a demonstration, becomes a revolutionary.

Cast: Jack Thompson, Carol Burns, Denis Lill, Elizabeth Watson, Michael Teen, Donna Akersten, Martyn Sanderson, Marshall Napier.

Crew: Screenplay: Andrew Brown (based on the book *Manhunt* by Howard Willis); Designer: Kai Hawkins; Photography: Gary Hanson; Music: Richard Hartley; Editor: Peter Hollywood.

Producer: Andrew Brown.

Director: Mike Newell.

Bad Blood

In this dramatic retelling of actual events in October 1941, Stan Graham (Thompson), a Westland smallholder, develops a persecution complex and starts to threaten his neighbours. They put up with it for a while but things become intolerable. When a party of four policemen arrives to confiscate his firearms, Graham is at a flashpoint — he loves his guns and isn't about to hand them over. He shoots and kills the four policemen and, in the ensuing altercations, three more locals, before heading to the hills. A manhunt composed of police, army and home guard is organised and tracks Graham down.

Goodbye Pork Pie

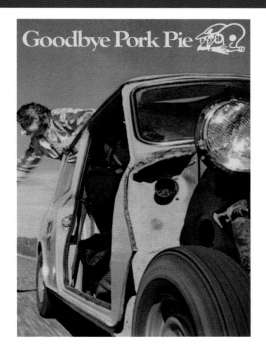

Cast: Tony Barry, Kelly Johnson, Claire Oberman, Shirley Gruar, John Bach, Bruno Lawrence.

Writers: Geoff Murphy, Ian Mune; Editor: Michael Horton; Photography: Alun Bollinger; Music: John Charles.

Producers: Geoff Murphy, Nigel Hutchinson.

Director: Geoff Murphy.

An out-of-work teenager (Johnson) finds a driver's licence and uses it to take a hire car for a joy ride south from Kaitaia. In Auckland, during an encounter with a traffic cop, a stranger (Barry) comes to his aid. The man's wife has just left him to travel to Invercargill 'to find her own space' and without money, the teenager and the hire car provide him with the means to follow her. Many madcap adventures ensue.

Race for the Yankee Zephyr

By chance a deer hunter (Wahl) and his bumbling partner (Pleasence) stumble upon the wreckage of a DC-3 on the shore of Lake Wakatipu. Included in its cargo are medals, booze, money and $50 million in gold bullion. Before they can begin recovery, others get wind of the discovery and show up to pressure them into revealing the location.

Cast: Ken Wahl, Lesley Ann Warren, Donald Pleasence, Bruno Lawrence, Grant Tilly, George Peppard.

Crew: Screenplay: Everett de Roche; Photography: Vincent Monton; Editor: John Laing; Composer: Brian May.

Producers: Antony Ginnane, John Barnett, David Hemmings.

Director: David Hemmings.

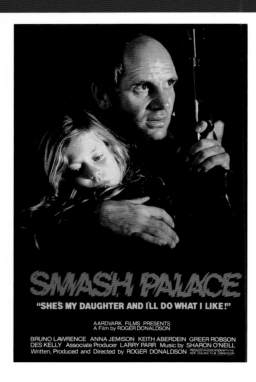

Smash Palace

Cast: Bruno Lawrence, Ana Jemison, Keith Aberdein, Greer Robson, Desmond Kelly.

Crew: Screenplay: Roger Donaldson, Peter Hansard, Bruno Lawrence; Photography: Graeme Cowley; Editor: Michael Horton; Music: Sharon O'Neill.

Producer and Director: Roger Donaldson.

Retired racing car driver Al (Lawrence), who now runs a wrecker's yard in Horopito, is more interested in his cars than his French wife (Jemison), who is like a fish out of water, having married him when he was racing on the international circuit. To Al's anger, she forms a relationship with his best friend, the local cop (Aberdein). When she finally leaves him, she takes their young daughter (Robson) with her. Al wants to keep his daughter and abducts her, heading into the bush and life on the run, but is forced to return to town when she becomes ill.

Cast: David Bowie, Tom Conti, Ryuichi Sakamoto, Beat Takeshi, Jack Thompson, Johnny Okura, Alistair Browning.

Crew: Screenplay: Nagisa Oshima with Paul Mayersberg, based on the book *The Seed and the Sower* by Laurens van der Post; Photography: Toichiro Narushima; Music: Ryuichi Sakamoto; Editor: Tomoyo Oshima.

Producer: Jeremy Thomas.

Director: Nagisa Oshima.

Merry Christmas Mr Lawrence

In 1942 Java, after the Japanese have invaded and taken British soldiers prisoner, beating and idiosyncratic Japanese practices are the new order. A New Zealand soldier (Bowie) is captured on a mission and brought into this environment where, in spite of the hostility, there is a strange attraction and interaction between jailers and prisoners.

Utu

Cast: Anzac Wallace, Bruno Lawrence, Wi Kuki Kaa, Tim Elliott, Kelly Johnson, John Bach, Tania Bristowe, Ilona Rodgers, Faenza Reuben, Martyn Sanderson, Merata Mita.

Crew: Screenplay: Geoff Murphy, Keith Aberdein; Photography: Graeme Cowley; Editing: Michael Horton, Ian John; Music: John Charles.

Producer and Director: Geoff Murphy.

New Zealand in 1870 — a friendly Maori village is massacred by colonial troops and discovered by army scout, Te Wheke (Wallace), whose people are among the dead. He turns on his employers and takes up his warrior past. Seeking utu (revenge), he engages in guerrilla warfare against the Pakeha. One of those attacked is a farmer (Lawrence) whose wife is killed and house burned. He in turns seeks his vengeance.

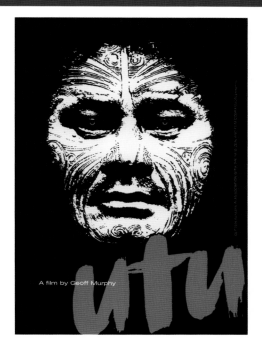

A film by Geoff Murphy

The Bounty

Based on the disastrous voyage of the HMS *Bounty*, this revisionist version of the mutinous tale offers new insight into the characters, particularly through its depiction and exoneration of Bligh. In this film, he is seen as a professional seaman who maintains an appropriate level of discipline, rather than as an outrageous tyrant. Under Bligh's (Hopkins) autocratic rule, the *Bounty* begins an ill-timed voyage around Cape Horn. The crew approach a breaking point, and Fletcher Christian (Gibson) leads them in revolt. But Christian fails to grasp the dire consequences that await them all.

Cast: Mel Gibson, Anthony Hopkins, Laurence Olivier, Daniel Day-Lewis, Liam Neeson, Edward Fox, Bernard Hill, Philip Davis.

Crew: Screenwriter: Robert Bolt, based on the book *Captain Bligh and Mr Christian* by Richard Hough; Photography: Arthur Ibbetson; Editor: Tony Lawson; Costume Designer: John Bloomfield; Composer: Vangelis.

Director: Roger Donaldson.

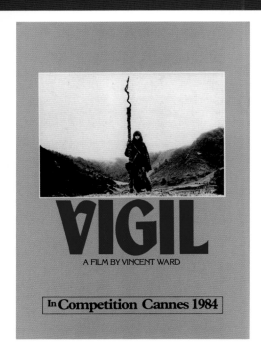

Vigil

Cast: Bill Kerr, Fiona Kay, Frank Whitten, Gordon Shields, Penelope Stewart.

Crew: Screenplay: Vincent Ward, Graham Tetley; Photography: Alun Bollinger; Editor: Simon Reece; Music: Jack Body.

Producer: John Maynard.

Director: Vincent Ward.

Toss (Kay), a solitary girl, lives in an isolated mist- and rain-soaked rural valley, whose reality is only slightly less haunting than her fantasies. When Toss's father dies in an accident, Ethan (Whitten), an itinerant hunter, wanders onto the family farm and is given a job by her grandfather. Toss's fairly innocent relationship with Ethan is severed when he forms a relationship with her mother (Stewart). The young girl matures quickly, with her fantasies growing increasingly malevolent.

The Rescue

Cast: Edward Albert, Ellen Barber, Timothy Carhart, James Cromwell, Anne E. Curry, Kevin Dillon, Ian Giatti, Charles Haid, Marc Price, Leon Russom.

Crew: Writers: John Thomas, Jim Thomas; Editors: David Holden, Carroll Timothy O'Meara; Production Design: Maurice Cain; Makeup: Rosalina Da Silva; Camera: Russell Boyd; Music: Bruce Broughton.

Producer: Barrie Melrose, Barrie M. Osborne, Laura Ziskin.

Director: Ferdinand Fairfax.

A team of Navy Seals is sent to destroy a disabled submarine to prevent it falling into the wrong hands. They complete their mission, but are captured before they can return to base. The U. S. Government refuses to mount a rescue mission to free the soldiers, so their teenage children take over. The kids must find a way to venture into the foreign country and overcome many obstacles.

The Quiet Earth

Cast: Bruno Lawrence, Alison Routledge, Peter Smith.

Crew: Writers: Bill Baer, Bruno Lawrence, Sam Pillsbury (based on the novel by Craig Harrison); Photography: James Bartle; Music: John Charles; Production Designer: Josephine Ford; Editor: Michael Horton.

Director: Geoff Murphy.

A scientist (Lawrence) wakes up one morning to discover the world is strangely silent — everyone has disappeared, thanks to a botched atomic experiment that has rendered the fabric of the galaxy unstable. At first he has fun doing anything he wants, but gradually isolation takes hold. Then he discovers he is not alone — two more survivors emerge to join him.

Willow

When young Willow Ufgood (Davis) finds an abandoned baby, he is suddenly thrust into an adventure filled with magic and danger. According to an ancient prophecy, the sacred child is destined to end the reign of the evil sorceress Queen Bavmorda (Marsh). Now, with only a single swordsman (Kilmer) at his side, Willow must overcome the forces of darkness that threaten to destroy anyone who stands in the Queen's way.

Cast: Val Kilmer, Joanne Whalley, Warwick Davis, Jean Marsh, Patricia Hayes, Billy Barty, Pat Roach, Gavan O'Herlihy, David Steinberg, Phil Fondacaro, Tony Cox, Robert Gillibrand, Mark Northover, Kevin Pollak, Rick Overton.

Crew: Writer: Bob Dolman on story by George Lucas; Music: James Horber; Editors: Daniel P Hanley, Michael Hill, Richard Hiscott; Costumes: Barbara Lane; Camera: Adrian Biddle.

Producers: Nigel Wooll, George Lucas.

Director: Ron Howard.

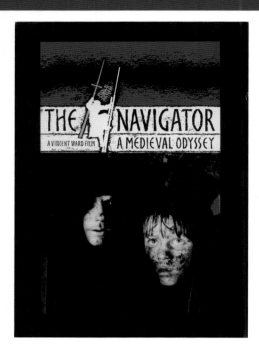

The Navigator

Cast: Bruce Lyons, Chris Haywood, Hamish McFarlane, Marshall Napier, Noel Appleby, Paul Livingston.

Crew: Screenplay: Vincent Ward, Kely Lyons, Geoff Chapple; Photography: Geoffrey Simpson; Editor: John Scott; Music: Davood Tabrizi; Production Designer: Sally Campbell.

Producers: Gary Hannam, John Maynard.

Director: Vincent Ward.

A mining village in England's Cumbria, in 1348 — the year of the Black Death — is the starting point for this medieval fantasy. A boy has a recurring dream about a city far away. If the villagers take copper and cast a cross for the cathedral spire of that city, the villagers will be saved from the advancing plague. One night the boy and five men set off down a shaft which leads them through space and time to the other side of the earth (New Zealand), but in the mid-1980s.

The Piano

Cast: Holly Hunter, Anna Paquin, Harvey Keitel, Sam Neill, Kerry Walker, Geneviève Lemon, Tungia Baker, Ian Mune.

Crew: Screenplay: Jane Campion; Photography: Stuart Dryburgh; Editor: Veronika Jenet; Music: Michael Nyman.

Producer: Jan Chapman.

Director: Jane Campion.

In the 1840s a mute Scottish woman (Hunter) makes the voyage from England to New Zealand, with her young daughter (Paquin), for a prearranged marriage. She brings with her a piano, as music is her refuge in a hostile and uninviting environment. Her arranged husband (Neill) is unimpressed with the piano and leaves it on the windswept beach, before swapping it with a neighbour (Keitel) for land. The neighbour bargains with the woman for the return of the piano — he will yield it to her in return for lessons, but he is motivated by romantic rather than musical interest.

An Angel at My Table

Cast: Kerry Fox, Alexia Keogh, Karen Fergusson, Iris Chum, Kevin J. Wilson, Melina Bernecker, Andrew Robertt, Glynis Angell, Sarah Smuts-Kennedy, Martyn Sanderson, David Letch, William Brandt.

Crew: Screenplay: Laura Jones; Production Design: Grant Major; Editor: Veronika Haeussler; Director of Photography: Stuart Dryburgh; Composer: Don McGlashan.

Producers: Bridgit Ikin, John Maynard.

Director: Jane Campion.

A biographical account of the life of Janet Frame (played in turn by Karen Fergusson, Alexia Keogh and Kerry Fox), a sweet-natured but painfully shy and insecure woman who battles schizophrenia, but goes on to become an acclaimed novelist. Based on the first book of Frame's award-winning autobiography of the same name, the film is hauntingly beautiful.

Heavenly Creatures

A re-telling of the notorious Parker-Hulme affair, one of New Zealand's most notable historic murder cases involving two teenage schoolgirls who murdered one of their mothers. The two girls, Juliet (Winslet) and Pauline (Lynskey) meet at school after Juliet has arrived with her parents from England, and quickly develop an intense and sexual relationship, which includes a shared fantasy world. When Juliet's parents plan a return to England, the girls assume they will be able to travel and live together, but when Pauline's mother refuses to allow her daughter to leave, the girls decided that eliminating her is the solution, and a bloody murder and sensational trial ensue.

Cast: Melanie Lynskey, Kate Winslet, Sarah Peirse, Diana Kent, Clive Merrison, Simon O'Connor.

Crew: Writers: Peter Jackson, Fran Walsh; Production Design: Grant Major; Director of Photography: Alun Bollinger; Editor: Jamie Selkirk; Music: Peter Dasent.

Producer: Jim Booth.

Director: Peter Jackson.

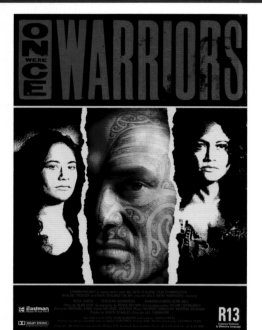

Once Were Warriors

Cast: Temuera Morrison, Rena Owen, Anita Kerr-Bell, Taungaroa Emile, Julian Arahanga, Rachael Morris, Cliff Curtis, Ray Bishop, Calvin Tuteao.

Crew: Screenplay: Riwia Brown (from the book by Alan Duff); Photography: Stuart Dryburg; Editor: Michael Horton; Music: Murray Grindlay, Murray McNabb, Herbs.

Producer: Robin Scholes.

Director: Lee Tamahori.

A hard-hitting drama based on the best-selling novel by Alan Duff, portraying a Maori family in the state-housing wasteland of South Auckland. Jake, the father (Morrison), rejected by his wife's tribe and laid off from work, contents himself by drinking with his mates in the local booze barn and partying at night. Like several of the men depicted, he's not slow to use his fists and boots on anyone who riles him, including his wife (Owen). During the film the oldest son is inducted into a gang, another son is put away for stealing, and the 13-year-old daughter (Kerr-Bell) commits suicide after being raped by her uncle (Curtis).

The Frighteners

Cast: Michael J. Fox, Trini Alvarado, Peter Dobson, John Astin, Dee Wallace-Stone, Jeffrey Combs, Jake Busey, Chi McBride.

Crew: Writers: Peter Jackson, Fran Walsh; Production Design: Grant Major; Directors of Photography: Alun Bollinger, John Blick; Editor: Jamie Selkirk; Music: Danny Elfman.

Executive Producer: Robert Zemekis.

Director: Peter Jackson.

In the quiet town of Fairwater, Frank Bannister (Fox) makes a living by ridding haunted houses of their unwelcome 'guest'. But, as it happens, he is in collusion with the very ghosts he promises to evict. It works well until he happens upon a case which involves a diabolical spirit on a murderous rampage — and to Frank's horror, his fellow townspeople think he is responsible.

Scarfies

Cast: Willa O'Neill, Neill Rea, Ashleigh Seagar, Taika Cohen, Charlie Bleakley, Jon Brazier.

Crew: Screenplay: Duncan Sarkies, Robert Sarkies; Director of Photography: Stephen Downes; Editor: Annie Collins; Sound Designer: Chris Burt.

Producer: Lisa Chatfield.

Director: Robert Sarkies.

This dark comedy is set in contemporary Dunedin, where a university student has found an old, large 'abandoned' house and invites other students to share. It even has running water and electricity, and they soon discover most of the basement is securely locked. It isn't long before someone forces it open and discovers a huge automated marijuana-growing operation. One of the students talks the others into harvesting the find and selling it to a dealer he knows — unleashing anarchy and mayhem when the real owner turns up.

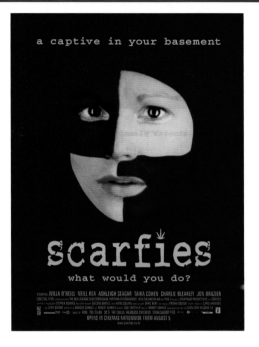

Vertical Limit

Cast: Nicholas Lea, Bill Paxton, Robin Tunney, Chris O'Donnell, Scott Glenn, Izabella Scorupco.

Crew: Writer: Robert King; Music: James Newton Howard; Camera: David Tattersall; Editor: Thom Noble; Production Design: Jon Bunker; Makeup: Nikki Gooley; Production Managers: Tim Coddington, Tink Ten Eyck, Julie Huntsinger; Sound: Valerie Davidson; Special Effects: Neil Corbould.

Producers: Martin Campbell, Robert King, Marcia Nasatir, Lloyd Phillips.

Director: Martin Campbell.

An ambitious mountain climber gives up the sport he loves after he and his sister are involved in the death of their father, during a climb. Though estranged from his sister, he is forced to jump into action again when she and her significant other run into difficulties while scaling K2, the second highest mountain in the world.

Perfect Strangers

Cast: Sam Neill, Rachael Blake, Joel Tobeck, Robyn Malcolm, Madeleine Sami, Paul Glover, Jed Brophy.

Crew: Screenplay: Gaylene Preston; Photography: Alun Bollinger; Editor: John Gilbert; Music: Plan 9 (David Donaldson, Janet Roddick and Stephen Roche); Production Designer: Joe Bleakley.

Producer: Robin Laing, Gaylene Preston.

Director: Gaylene Preston.

Melanie (Blake) is lonely, living in a small town, working in a dead-end job and in need of male companionship. She meets a man (Neill) at a local pub and agrees to go back to his boat, where she drinks too much and passes out. When she awakes, she finds the boat is headed out to sea.

Cast: Elijah Wood, Sir Ian McKellen, Liv Tyler, Viggo Mortensen, Sean Astin, Cate Blanchett, John Rhys-Davies, Billy Boyd, Christopher Lee, Dominic Monaghan, Orlando Bloom, Miranda Otto, Bernard Hill, Andy Serkis, David Wenham, Sir Ian Holm, Sean Bean.

Crew: Director of Photography: Andrew Lesnie; Creature, Miniature, Armour, and Special Make-up Effects Supervisor: Richard Taylor; Film Editors: Michael Horton, John Gilbert; Production Designer: Grant Major; Costume Designer: Ngila Dickson.

Producers: Peter Jackson, Barrie M. Osborne, Fran Walsh, Tim Sanders (FOTR only).

Director: Peter Jackson.

Executive Producers: Robert Shaye, Michael Lynne, Mark Ordesky, Bob and Harvey Weinstein.

The Lord of the Rings Trilogy:

The Fellowship of the Ring
The Two Towers
The Return of the King

The Dark Lord Sauron seeks to enslave the free peoples of the realm of Middle-earth by recovering a mighty ring of power he forged in the fires beneath Mount Doom. After many generations, the ruling ring, cut from Sauron's hand by the human hero Isildur, has fallen by chance into the keeping of the Hobbit Bilbo Baggins (Holm). A Fellowship of Men (Mortensen and Bean), an Elf Lord (Bloom) a Dwarf (Rhys-Davies) and four Hobbits (Wood, Boyd, Monaghan and Astin) guided by the Wizard Gandalf (McKellen) embark on a perilous quest to destroy the Ring before Sauron's minions can recapture it.

Rain

Cast: Alicia Fulford-Wierzbicki, Sarah Peirse, Marton Csokas, Alistair Browning, Aaron Murphy.

Crew: Screenplay: Christine Jeffs from a novel by Kirsty Gunn; Art Director: Kirsty Clayton; Director of Photography: John Toon; Editor: Paul Maxwell; Music: Neil Finn and Edmund McWilliams.

Executive Producer: Robin Scholes.

Producer: Philippa Campbell.

Director: Christine Jeffs.

It is late summer in the 1970s with 13-year-old Janey and her family, who are settling into their Northland east coast cottage for another seaside holiday. Her days are full of swimming and fishing. At night her parents give parties where the adults drink, dance and flirt, but as the holiday continues Janey becomes increasingly aware of the cracks in her parents' marriage. Watching her mother begin an affair with a visiting photographer, Janey begins to discover her own sexuality, and decides to grow up quickly.

Without a Paddle

When three young guys take a canoe into the Oregon wilderness in search of lost treasure, everything that can go wrong does. Hunted by two backwoods dope farmers, they encounter death-defying rapids, tree-hugging hippie chicks and a crazy old mountain man (Reynolds).

Cast: Seth Green, Matthew Lillard, Dax Shepard, Ethan Suplee, Abraham Benrubi, Rachel Blanchard, Burt Reynolds.

Crew: Art Directors: Simon Bright, Denise Hudson; Production Designer: Perry Andelin Blake; Music: Christopher Beck; Costume Designer: Ngila Dickson; Editors: Debra Neil-Fisher, Peck Prior; Camera: Jonathan Brown.

Producer: Donald De Line.

Director: Steven Brill.

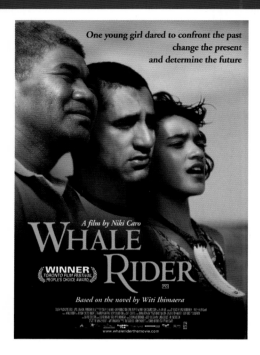

One young girl dared to confront the past change the present and determine the future

A film by Niki Caro

WHALE RIDER

WINNER
TORONTO FILM FESTIVAL
PEOPLE'S CHOICE AWARD

Based on the novel by Witi Ihimaera

www.whaleriderthemovie.com

Whale Rider

Cast: Keisha Castle-Hughes, Rawiri Paratene, Vicky Haughton, Cliff Curtis, Grant Roa, Mana Taumaunu, Rachel House, Taungaroa Emile.

Crew: Screenplay: Niki Caro from a novel by Witi Ihimaera; Director of Photography: Leon Narbey; Music: Lisa Gerrard; Editing: David Coulson; Costume Design: Kirsty Cameron; Production Design: Grant Major.

Producers: John Barnett, Frank Hüber, Tim Sanders.

Director: Niki Caro.

Executive Producers: Bill Gavin, Linda Goldstein Knowlton.

The people of Whangara believe their first ancestor, Paikea, arrived on the back of a whale, and a line of first-born boys has descended from him to become rangatira or traditional leader. When twins are born to the rangatira's only son (Curtis), the boy and his mother die in childbirth, leaving his daughter, Pai (Castle-Hughes). Her fiercely proud grandfather (Paratene) cannot accept his son's decision to have no more children and refuses to acknowledge either her claim or her love for him, despite the best efforts of his wife (Haughton).

Cast: Ken Watanabe, Tom Cruise, William Atherton, Chad Lindberg, Ray Goodshall Sr, Billy Connolly, Tony Goldwyn, Masato Harada, Masashi Odate, John Koyama, Timothy Spall, Schichinosuke Nakamura, Togo Igawa, Satosi Nikaido, Shintaro Wada.

Crew: Screenplay: John Logan; Editors: Victor Du Bois, Steven Rosenblum; Costume Designer: Ngila Dickson; Sound Editor: Randy Kelley; Production Designer: Lilly Kilvert; Camera: John Toll.

Producers: Tom Cruise, Tom Engelman, Marshall Herskovitz, Scott Kroopf, Paula Wagner, Edward Zwick.

Director: Edward Zwick.

The Last Samurai

Civil War hero Captain Nathan Algren (Cruise) is a man adrift. In the years since the Civil War, the world has changed. Pragmatism has replaced courage, self-interest has taken the place of sacrifice and honour is nowhere to be found.

A universe away, Katsumoto (Watanabe) is the last leader of an ancient line of Samurai warriors. Their paths converge when the young Emperor of Japan hires Algren to train Japan's first modern army. But as the Emperor's advisors attempt to eradicate the Samurai, Algren finds himself impressed — their powerful convictions remind him of the man he once was. Thrust into harsh and unfamiliar territory, with his life in the balance, the troubled American finds himself at the centre of a violent and epic struggle between two worlds, with only his sense of honour to guide him.

The World's Fastest Indian

Cast: Anthony Hopkins, Jessica Cauffiel, Saginaw Grant, Diane Ladd, Christopher Lawford, Aaron Murphy, Paul Rodriguez, Annie Whittle, Chris Williams, Chris Bruno, Carlos Lacamara, Patrick Flueger, Walton Goggins, Bruce Greenwood, Joe Howard.

Crew: Art Direction: Roger Guise, Mark Hofeling; Production Design: Robert Gillies, J. Dennis Washington; Editor: John Gilbert; Visual Effects Supervisor: Kent Houston; Camera: David Gribble.

Producers: Roger Donaldson, Gary Hannam.

Director: Roger Donaldson.

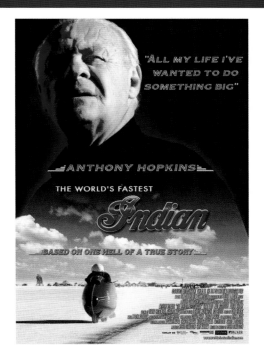

The inspiring true story of New Zealand motorcycling legend Burt Munro (Hopkins) is told with warmth and whimsy. After a lifetime of perfecting his classic Indian motorcycle, an elderly Burt set off from Invercargill to test his bike at the Bonneville Salt Flats in Utah. Against all odds, he not only made it to Bonneville, but managed to convince sceptical organisers that his homemade machine was safe to ride. He not only completed the course, he set a 1967 speed record that remains unbroken today.

Perfect Creature

For 300 years vampires — the Church of the Brotherhood — and human beings have lived in peaceful co-existence; the vampire Brothers are not the horrific creatures of myth, but the next step in human evolution. But the discovery of the Brothers has also led to early genetic experiments and ever since humanity has been assailed by virulent plagues. *Perfect Creature* is a highly original retelling of the vampire myth, set in an alternative version of the 1960s. Science fiction and horror coalesce in a suspenseful, elegant, action film about race, serial killings and the capacity of human beings to hope.

Cast: Dougray Scott, Saffron Burrows, Leo Gregory, Scott Wills, Stuart Wilson, Craig Hall, Robbie Magasiva, Lauren Jackson, Peter McCauley, Stephen Ure, John Sumner, Roi Taimana, Danielle Cormack, Aaron Murphy, Scott Morrison.

Crew: Production Manager: Moira Grant; Art Direction: Nick Bassett, Robert Bavin; Editor: Chris Blunden; Music: Anne Dudley.

Producers: Michael Cowan, Russel Fischer, Jason Piette, Tim Sanders, Haneet Vaswani.

Director: Glenn Standring.

River Queen

Cast: Samantha Morton, Kiefer Sutherland, Cliff Curtis, Temuera Morrison, Anton Lesser, Rawiri Pene, Stephen Rea, Wi Kuki Kaa, Mark Ruka, Tyson Reweti, Grayson Putu, Nathan Passfield, Laura Coyte Douglas, Julie Ranginui, Brandon Lakshman.

Crew: Editor: Ewa J. Lind; Production Designer: Rick Kofoed; Costume: Barbara Darragh; Art Director: Shayne Radford; Sound: Peter Baldock; Visual Effects: Cheryl Bainum.

Producers: Chris Auty; Don Reynolds.

Director: Vincent Ward.

New Zealand, 1868. Sarah O'Brien (Morton) has grown up in a frontier garrison. She gives birth to a son (Pene) by a Maori father and seven years later, he is kidnapped by his Maori grandfather. Abandoned by her own father (Rea), Sarah searches for her son, her only friend Doyle (Sutherland), a broken-down soldier. Lured to the village of the rebel chief Te Kai Po (Morrison), Sarah falls for Boy's uncle, Wiremu (Curtis), and the Maori way of life. Sarah heals Te Kai Po but her life is shattered when she realises he plans to declare war on the Colonials.

Cast: Georgie Henley, Skandar Keynes, Tilda Swinton, William Moseley, Anna Popplewell, James McAvoy, Jim Broadbent, Kiran Shah, James Cosmo, Judy McIntosh, Elizabeth Hawthorne, Patrick Kake, Shane Rangi.

Crew: Editors: Sim Evan-Jones, Jim May; Production Design: Roger Ford; Art Direction: Ian Gracie; Makeup: Nikki Gooley; Production Managers: Tim Coddington, Beth DePatie; Production Sound Mixer: Tony Johnston; Special Effects Director: Dean Wright; Music: Harry Gregson-Williams.

Producers: Andrew Adamson, Mark Johnson, Philip Steuer.

Director: Andrew Adamson.

The Chronicles of Narnia: The Lion, The Witch and The Wardrobe

In the first movie adaptation of C. S. Lewis' classic, *The Chronicles of Narnia*, the story begins in World War II England, when Lucy (Henley), Edmund (Keynes), Susan (Popplewell) and Peter (Moseley) enter the world of Narnia through a magical wardrobe while playing a game of hide-and-seek in the country home of an elderly professor. Once there, the children discover a charming, peaceful land inhabited by talking beasts: dwarfs, fauns, centaurs and giants — whose world has been cursed with eternal winter by the evil White Witch, Jadis (Swinton). Under the guidance of a noble and mystical ruler, the lion Aslan, the children fight to overcome the White Witch's powerful hold over Narnia.

King Kong

In Peter Jackson's 2005 remake of the classic movie of the same name, Ann Darrow (Watts), an actress from the world of vaudeville, finds herself out of a job in Depression-era New York. Her luck changes when she meets Carl Denham (Black). Denham is an entrepreneur, raconteur, adventurer and filmmaker struggling to make his name in the entertainment industry. Bold, ebullient and charismatic, Denham has a natural sense of showmanship and an appetite for greatness, which ultimately leads to catastrophe.

Meanwhile, Jack Driscoll (Brody), a New York playwright, finds his heart and physical courage are put to the test when Black kidnaps him on a voyage to film the mysterious Skull Island, inhabited by giant dinosaurs and the last of a race of giant apes — Kong. After a series of incredible and dramatic adventures, the giant ape is captured and brought back to civilisation, and to a tragic end after he escapes and runs amok amongst the skyscrapers of New York.

Cast: Naomi Watts, Jack Black, Adrien Brody, Thomas Kretschmann, Colin Hanks, Andy Serkis, Evan Parke, Jamie Bell, Lobo Chan, John Sumner, Craig Hall, Kyle Chandler, Bill Johnson, Mark Hadlow, Geraldine Brophy.

Crew: Music: James Newton Howard; Camera: Andrew Lesnie, Derek Whipple; Editor: Jamie Selkirk; Production Design: Grant Major; Art Direction: Simon Bright, Dan Hennah; Costume Design: Terry Ryan; Makeup: Rick Findlater; Production Managers: Belindalee Hope, Brigitte York; Sound: Mike Hopkins.

Producers: Jan Blenkin, Carolynne Cunningham, Peter Jackson, Fran Walsh.

Director: Peter Jackson.

North Island
locations

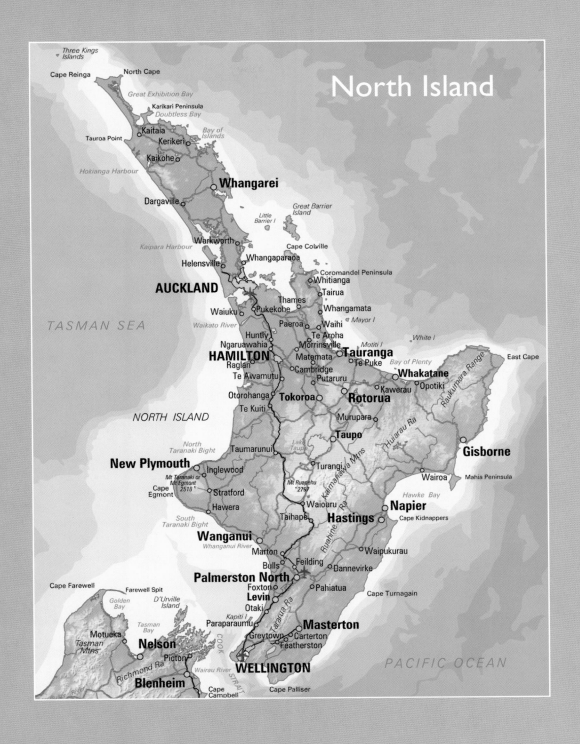

North Island

Northland

Internet: www.northlandnz.com

Who needs an overseas tropical resort? Unspoilt Matai Bay at the top end of the Karikari Peninsula oozes relaxation.

The main street of Kaitaia has changed little since Gerry found a driver's licence and began his drive to Invercargill.

Kaitaia is the most northern town in New Zealand, with some of the oldest traces of Maori settlement, where Northland iwi claim Kupe (the legendary explorer who sailed the South Pacific) made his first landfall in nearby Hokianga Harbour.

European settlers arrived in the late eighteenth century and the township began as whalers and sealers plied their trade. Kauri logging and the extraction of kauri gum soon followed, and a colourful era of Dalmatian settlement helped give the area some of its distinctive flavour. A subtropical climate is evident in the lush vegetation growth of the winterless north.

In **Goodbye Pork Pie** Gerry Austin commenced his legendary journey from the main street of Kaitaia. 'Borrowing' a distinctive yellow mini for a journey to Auckland he leaves the area — heading south. Although the movie doesn't record which of the two available routes south Gerry followed, we will assume he went the scenic route via Awanui and Mangonui.

At nearby Awanui the Ancient Kauri Kingdom is well worth a stop. Kauri is one of the finest timbers in the world, with a distinctive grain and a deep golden hue. Here, ancient logs that have lain buried for thousands of years are recovered and crafted into beautiful pieces of furniture and wooden products. Awanui also marks the departure point to the tip of the North Island at Cape Reinga.

Continuing on SH10, the Karikari Peninsula is signposted further northeast and is host to Matai Bay, one of the most beautiful beaches in the area. Returning to the main highway, continue via Kerikeri and Paihia before reaching SH1 at Kawakawa.

The lure of big-game fishing brings people to Whangaroa Harbour, also a popular port of call for yachts from around the world.

Cable Bay was named in 1902 when the longest cable in the world stretched from here to Queensland in Australia.

The small town of Kawakawa houses a lasting memorial to internationally renowned artist and architect, Frederick Hundertwasser, who fell in love with Northland. In 1998 he designed a new toilet block in the main street, the only example of his work in the Southern Hemisphere and one of the world's most photographed 'loos'.

Rain making

Just 50 km north of Auckland, the Kawau Bay, Leigh and Tawharanui area offers a huge range of marine recreational environments — beaches, bays, harbours, wrecks and islands. While the novel *Rain* is set on the shores of Lake Taupo, director Christine Jeffs moved the film setting north for a number of reasons, both aesthetic and logistical. We needed to be close to a city with a film industry (for film labs, crew and technical stuff) and a seaside with beaches, a boat harbour and islands. Christine and I live in the area and found some of the locations on horseback while riding the Omaha estuary at low tide (the boat yard and the 'will you dance with me' beach party scene). The rest were found in a panic just weeks before we shot. We knew it was all here, as I had scouted the whole area by chopper for a commercial the year before. It was just a matter of nutting out the details of the film's world and getting the various permissions.

There isn't much in the way of sophisticated accommodation in these parts, so our cast and crew were housed in local holiday homes rented for the shoot, as were the production office and cutting room. Some of the crew lived right on the water in Scandrettes Bay, the main shooting location.

Casting from Warkworth was very successful, we found almost all our children locally, and eight-year-old Aaron Murphy (Jim) was cast from the local school.

All the water scenes were shot on the *Brenda Lee* with one bigger support boat, both rented locally, and several rubber duck safety boats from the Omaha surf club. The area is very tidal and scheduling for light, tide as well as the other stuff scheduling requires was complex, the whole unit almost awash on occasion. The movie was shot later in the year than planned but we had no weather issues. We started just before Easter and shot for 32 days. All the interiors were shot in the actual locations, which gave us greater flexibility with the schedule. I'm not sure if we ever had a rainy day. The worst weather was the night of the naked swimming scene, where the kids see Kate make out with Cady. In fact, the only weather issue we had was the sound of water lapping outside — on windy days this gave the sound department a few headaches. We all enjoyed working in the area and the area truly worked well for us.

John Toon ACS
Cinematographer / Associate Producer

Warkworth and the Mahurangi Peninsula

Internet:
www.warkworth-information.co.nz

Situated 90 minutes north of Auckland, the Mahurangi Peninsula is a very popular holiday destination for those wishing to swap the city for some sun and surf — and it was this exact combination that appealed to the production crew for *Rain*. As producer Philippa Campbell saw it: 'It's a landscape that hasn't been explored in depth in a feature film until now. A place of incredible beauty.'

The small beach of typical holiday homes at Sandspit looking across a broad bay is reached from Warkworth, a township that retains its village appeal. Good shopping, excellent cafés and galleries make Warkworth a great stop en route.

When New Zealand writer Kirsty Gunn published her first novel *Rain* in 1994, it received international acclaim. Christine Jeffs, director of *Rain*, loved the sense of atmosphere and foreboding in the novel and its reflection on childhood. Her particular challenge was to recreate those elements on film, and she spent a long time trying to persuade others this was a story about the detail of everyday life, worth translating to the screen.

Heading south on SH1, turn left at Thompson Road for the Warkworth Satellite Receiving Station. Opened in 1971, the station allowed international news to be beamed live to New Zealand as well as enabling increased telephone and radio access. In 1985, director Geoff Murphy used this station in *The Quiet Earth*.

Below right: Scott Point at the tip of the Mahurangi Peninsula has a very sheltered beach and the historic Scott Homestead built in 1877. Maori have occupied this area for centuries and there are many accessible archaeological sites.

Below: The satellite dish near Warkworth was used to portray the scientific base that caused all the problems in *The Quiet Earth*.

Auckland

Internet:
www.aucklandnz.com

Home to one-third of New Zealand's population, Auckland sits astride the Waitemata and Manukau Harbours — a multicultural and commercial city of beaches and urban sprawl.

After the signing of the Treaty of Waitangi in 1840, local iwi Ngati Whatua approached Captain William Hobson (the Lieutenant Governor of New Zealand) and requested he establish the new colonial capital in this area, which was named after Hobson's naval commander. In 1842 the first of many immigrants arrived and now the city thrives on a diverse mix of European and Polynesian cultures, with the world's largest Polynesian population.

Known as the City of Sails, the Waitemata Harbour reflects another world-beating statistic — Kiwis own more boats per head of population than anywhere else, and year-round fleets of yachts and boats sail and race in the harbour and visit the islands of the Hauraki Gulf. Downtown, the Viaduct Basin has hosted two America's Cup defences and is home to a feast of restaurants and bars. The nearby Maritime Museum is well worth a visit.

The many volcanic cones that dot the skyline of Auckland are peaceful oases in the urban landscape. Mt Eden commands wonderful views of the city and, while the iconic One Tree Hill (of U2 fame) is treeless after it was attacked as a political protest, it hasn't been renamed no tree hill yet! The surrounding Cornwall Park is a wonderful place to stroll amongst trees or climb the cone, complete with remnants of Maori pa (fortified villages).

The city of Auckland as seen over the top of an 8" disappearing gun on North Head, which guarded Auckland from the 1880s. The barrel weighs over 13 tons and the gun is a survivor of the days when North Head was one of a number of coastal forts built to defend Auckland from a feared Russian attack. Part of Auckland's coastal defence during both World Wars, the area is now an historic reserve and makes for a great afternoon's exploration.

Pine needles create a carpet under pine tree stumps in Woodhill Forest.

Known as toi toi (Maori for plant) or Prince of Wales Feathers, the plumed white flowers of this iconic grass are a significant part of the landscape in New Zealand, where most children have memories of using the long flower stems in their games.

An hour northwest of Auckland, the dark trees of Woodhill Forest were transformed into the camp of Jadis, the dreaded White Witch of Narnia in **The Chronicles of Narnia: The Lion, The Witch and The Wardrobe**.

The general area can be found by turning left onto Rimmer Road (clearly signposted off SH16 before Helensville) and travelling into the forest. The forest also has a network of mountain-bike trails for riders of all levels.

Whilst in the area, a visit to Muriwai Beach is well worth the 30-minute diversion, with its black sand and waves from the Tasman Sea a favourite with surfers and holidaymakers. Otakamiro Point, at the southern end of the beach, is home to one of New Zealand's few mainland gannet-breeding colonies.

If sampling New Zealand wine is more of a priority, West Auckland is home to a number of vineyards.

Karekare Beach is a typical wild west coach beach with black sand and raging surf. A favourite with locals, its fame spread world-wide when it became one of the major stars of **The Piano**. The beach has also appeared in various episodes of **Xena: Warrior Princess**.

The area was milled extensively last century for kauri and remains of the bush railways can still be seen. There are a number of walks in the area and the beach makes an ideal picnic lunch spot. The wild water is great for surfing and fishing, but be aware it can have a dangerous rip at times.

To get to the beach, travel to Glen Eden and get onto the West Coast Road. Continue along to Piha Road before following the sign-posted road to Karekare.

The outside-in architecture of the Civic Theatre has entertained movie-goers for over 70 years.

Queen Street is the main shopping thoroughfare of Auckland city, with its harbour end marked by two historic buildings — The Ferry Building and the old Chief Post Office. Modelled in the Imperial Baroque style, the Ferry Building (99 Quay Street) was erected in 1909–12 as the hub for the many ferry services crossing the harbour. Today it is also home to many bars, restaurants and cafés.

Construction of the nearby Chief Post Office (12 Queen Street) was undertaken at the same time, with the Imperial Baroque style carried out in white Oamaru stone and Coromandel granite. In 2001 it was renovated and became part of the new city bus and rail terminus.

It was around this building that Bullen and Gloria were caught up in the riots in **Sleeping Dogs**. Many of these streets were also filmed as a deserted and lonely landscape as Zac Hobson tried to find another human being in **The Quiet Earth**.

Further up Queen Street is the Civic Theatre (cnr Wellesley Street) built in 1929 and now the largest surviving atmospheric cinema in Australasia. Atmospheric cinemas feature a fantastical interior specifically designed to transport the patron to faraway worlds as part of the cinema experience. The Civic features an Indian design throughout, complete with elephants, tigers, seated Buddhas and domed ceilings. Its arched roof of twinkling stars is another notable feature. The building is still a working theatre, and in 2004 extras in 1930s garb filled its interior with Peter Jackson and his crew, and moviegoers saw it systematically destroyed as a rampant King Kong tried to escape his captors.

Situated at 132 Beach Road is the former Auckland Railway Station, one of the largest and most ornate in the country. Built in 1929–30, the station was the main long-haul transportation centre in Auckland until the 1960s, when cars, trucks and aeroplanes began to dominate transportation. Three stories high, and complete with large waiting rooms, dining rooms and public areas, the building has a very similar style to American stations. Now the building has been converted to student accommodation for the nearby Auckland university and polytech campuses.

It was up the sweeping driveway, complete with Asian stalls, in *Merry Christmas Mr Lawrence* that Major Jack Celliers walked to his interrogation, which took place in the interior.

Nearby, the chic shopping area of Parnell provides an entrance to the Auckland Domain. This stately park is the oldest in Auckland and was developed around the cone of an extinct volcano. Specimen trees dating back to the 1850s provide the best shade from the hot Auckland summer, whilst formal gardens complete with statuary and ponds provide a very pleasant place for a stroll.

Situated in the gardens is the Auckland War Memorial Museum, which houses a priceless collection of Maori and Pacific treasures and up-to-the-minute interactive displays, including a very striking and memorable reinactment of a volcanic eruption.

The Wintergarden complex in the domain was established after World War I and consists of two display glasshouses, a formal courtyard with pond and a fernery built within an old quarry.

It was here in the formal courtyard that Major Celliers was brutally beaten in *Merry Christmas Mr Lawrence*.

The memorial to The Glorious Dead outside the Auckland War Memorial Museum. Every year on Anzac Day (25 April), thousands attend the Dawn Parade to pay their respects and remember those who died defending this country.

The main courtyard of the Wintergarden is a popular place for wedding photographs and with visitors who come to view the many exotic plants on display in the hothouses.

Coromandel

Internet:
www.thecoromandel.com

Above: An old wringer washing machine sits astride the elegant shop frontages in the main street of Coromandel.

Below right: The calm waters stretch across to Turkey Island, home of Smith in *Sleeping Dogs*.

Below: The boatshed and wharf Smith rowed to at Kikowhakarere Bay, in *Sleeping Dogs*.

Situated 90 minutes from the bustle of Queen Street is the bush and beach playground of the Coromandel Peninsula. Driving south from Auckland, the Bombay Hills are soon behind you and on the wide Hauraki Plains tree-covered mountains edge around the horizon.

The historic town of Thames marks the entrance to the peninsula. In the late nineteenth century, the town was one of the largest in New Zealand, as prospectors sought their fortune in gold and kauri-logging. Today, the town combines modern malls with an historic main street and character boutiques.

The drive north to Coromandel township initially follows the coast line past tranquil bays and small holiday homes before crossing hills of subtropical forest before a final descent into the seaside township.

The village is host to a number of cafés serving local seafood. For a wonderful picnic lunch, visit the Coromandel Smoking Company and stock up with succulent smoked fish and fresh oysters before travelling to one of the many beaches.

Kikowhakarere Bay is situated 14 km north of Coromandel. From the beach look across to Motupohukuo (Turkey) Island. Here Smith lived in *Sleeping Dogs*, rowing to the small jetty at the northern end of the bay. Drive 1 km further north and stop at the top of the hill. There is a great view of the island as well as a track down to beautiful unspoilt Oamaru Beach. The cast and crew of *Sleeping Dogs* spent many days swimming and partying here during filming.

From Coromandel the road to the eastern shores is a climb over the spine of the peninsula before passing Kuaotunu and arriving in the main town on the peninsula —Whitianga.

Above: Kikowhakarere Bay with its small collection of holiday homes is perfectly sheltered and is a great place for a summer lunch under the shade of a pohutukawa.

Right: Known as the New Zealand Christmas tree because of its December flowering, the pohutukawa can be seen near most beaches in the North Island as their interweaving roots stretch out looking for water.

Below: A wonderful view of the area can be seen by taking the narrow-gauge Driving Creek Railway, a ten-minute drive from Coromandel. Featuring two spirals, three short tunnels, five reversing points and several large viaducts, the railway climbs 172 m above sea level.

Rotorua

Internet: www.rotoruanz.com

Heading south from Whitianga via the popular beach of Whangamata, a detour to the thermal city of Rotorua is a must. The heartland of a number of Maori iwi, Rotorua's diverse range of physical and cultural attractions have made the city one of the most visited tourist sites in New Zealand since late in the nineteenth century. The Pink and White Terraces, extraordinary natural silica formations, were praised in their day as the eighth natural wonder of the world, until their destruction in 1886 in a catastrophic volcanic eruption.

Early filmmakers in New Zealand were also captured by the allure of Rotorua, with Maori legends providing a rich source of inspiration, with a number of films produced in the region.

A Maori carving at Ohinemutu, home to Tamatekapua, captain of the Arawa canoe that brought Maori to New Zealand circa 1350AD.

Opened in 1908, the Bath House in Rotorua is a New Zealand tourist icon. Now home to the Rotorua Museum, the history and heritage of this area are brought alive in innovative ways.

St Faith's Church on the skyline at Ohinemutu.

Travelling eastward, the Bay of Plenty is home to Tauranga and Mt Maunganui, two of the fastest-growing cities in New Zealand. The area was given its bountiful name rather belatedly by Captain Cook in 1769, in tribute to the plentiful resources his men found here — local Maori had beaten him to the rich harvest of land and sea by over 700 years.

During the summer months both towns explode with visitors who come to enjoy the mild climate, beaches and relaxed lifestyle.

Situated at 81 Truman Road in Mount Maunganui is Bay Park Raceway. A 470 m track plays host to speedway and motor-racing events with raised stands to seat 17,500 people. The venue may have changed and grown since Shaw raced here in *Smash Palace* but the excitement still remains and Bay Park is a must for any speed enthusiast.

Tauranga

Internet: www.bayofplentynz.com

Left top: The main feature of the beach at Mt Maunganui is the 232-m high mountain at the entrance to Tauranga Harbour. The gentle harbour side of the beach is ideal for a sailing or kayaking lesson.

Left bottom: Adventure activities abound in this country. Commercial rafting down the Okere River located 21 km from Rotorua on SH83 features one of the highest drops.

Below: The surf beach at Mt Maunganui is popular with surfers, volleyball players and those in search of the sun, under the watchful eye of surf lifesavers.

East Coast

Internet: www.gisbornenz.com

The journey from Whakatane in the north to Gisborne in the south via East Cape is a mixture of beautiful scenery, remoteness and culture.

The area surrounding Opotiki (1 hour south of Whakatane) is rich in history. Two chiefs, Tarawa and Tuwharanui, set sail for New Zealand in their canoe accompanied by two fish known as O-Potiki-Mai-Tawhiti (two pets from afar). On landing the pair were placed in a nearby spring which was named after them, later abbreviated by English settlers to Opotiki.

During the Land Wars a number of engagements were fought in the area and a military garrison was established. After the fighting the land was settled by many semi-retired servicemen who farmed and remained on active call-up.

Continuing towards Hicks Bay there are many views of the Pacific Ocean, used by Roger Donaldson in **The Bounty**. The gleaming white Anglican Church at Raukokore is well worth a visit.

An overnight stay at Hicks Bay is recommended before travelling on to Gisborne. As the road alternates between beaches and bush-covered mountains, many small villages appear along the way. At Tolaga Bay pause to visit the historic wharf, believed to be the longest in the Southern Hemisphere. The 660m Ferro-concrete landmark was built in the 1920s to allow the berthing of larger ships, but by the 1950s land transport had taken over and the wharf soon languished. It is now being restored to its former glory.

Along the way you pass through the small village of Whangara, where **Whale Rider** was filmed.

As they have done for centuries, children fish near the wharf at Gisborne.

Paikea, the original Whale Rider.

I think one of the most exciting things about **Whale Rider** is its international resonance — the themes are relevant in all sorts of societies and cultures throughout the world. I approached the adaptation from the point of view of somebody who was once a 12-year-old girl . . . One thing that's important to know about this film is that it was really collaborative with the iwi. There is no way you can make a film like this and not be. The film is so rich because of their involvement, in so many ways.

There was secrecy around it because we didn't want anybody coming down and taking pictures and blowing our gig. We were trying to do something that in cinematic terms is really hard — whale strandings. These highly emotional and moving scenes with big pieces of fibreglass! There were lots of other challenges emotionally and culturally. Physically, it was a very intense shoot, but everybody was hugely supportive of the story and that made it a joy really.

Niki Caro, Director, **Whale Rider** (On Film)

This novel was set in Whangara and it would almost have been heresy to shoot anywhere else. There are physical things that are described in the book — the sweep of the bay, the island that looks like a whale, the meeting houses, and of course, the people whose legend we were telling. If we'd gone somewhere else and tried to manufacture the surroundings and the ambience, then I think it would have been noticeable in the picture.

John Barnett, Producer, **Whale Rider** (On Film)

The beach at Whangara.

Shops at Tokomaru Bay show a legacy from the past.

Napier

Internet
www.hawkesbaynz.com
www.artdeconapier.com

Established in 1851, Mission Estate is New Zealand's oldest winery. The historic seminary building, which houses a shop and restaurant, is the ideal spot for lunch and an excellent vintage.

Opened in 1936, the Tom Parker Fountain was modelled on a similar example in Bournemouth. Behind the fountain is Pania of the Reef, a statue modelled on a Maori story. Lured by the sirens of the sea, Pania swam out to meet them, but when she tried to return she was transformed into an offshore reef.

The cities of Napier and Hastings are a delight. Situated on the sweeping border of Poverty Bay, their temperate climate is only outmatched by their architecture and wine.

In 1931, an earthquake of magnitude 7.8 struck Hawke's Bay. Within minutes, 258 people were killed and the centre of Napier was totally destroyed in New Zealand's largest natural disaster.

Napier was rebuilt in the popular Art Deco style of the times, and the city remains as one of the most original of that style in the world today. Walking and driving tours are available to help you appreciate the beautiful and elegant architecture of the city and its surrounds.

Wine has been produced in this region of hot summers and cool winters for over 100 years, with over 4000 ha planted in grapes. A day spent visiting the many outstanding vineyards and their fine restaurants is highly recommended.

In 1982 Director Geoff Murphy and his crew arrived in the area to film *Utu*, the story of Maori fighting to keep their land from colonial settlement. Filming was undertaken near the main highway between Napier and Taupo at Te Pohue and Titiokura.

In Eskdale, pause at the beautifully restored church and then continue for approximately 25 minutes to Te Pohue. For keen golfers, the course is well worth playing. Titiokura is a further 15 minutes away on a road that climbs for magnificent views of the surrounding area.

You can continue to Taupo via this route but, if you are following this guide, return to Napier. Taupo will be visited later.

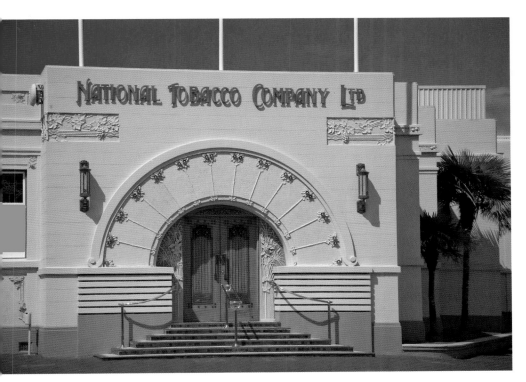

Above: Typical Art Deco colours and forms abound in Napier and Hastings, a pleasing change from modern glass edifices.

Left: Designed by Louis Hay, the Rothman's Building (now the National Tobacco Company) at Ahuriri epitomises Art Deco Napier.

Below: A short drive from Hastings will take you 400 m above sea level to Te Mata Peak. On a fine day the 360°-view takes in the Ruahine, Kaweka and Maungaharuru Ranges as well as the gannet colony at Cape Kidnappers.

The Wairarapa

Internet:
www.wairarapanz.com

The Wairarapa is an hour north of Wellington, and a popular destination, with spectacular landscapes, vineyards and a diverse range of adventure activities and tourist trails.

One of New Zealand's most unusual geographical landscapes can be seen at the Putangirua Pinnacles on the south coast of the Wairarapa, which were used in *The Return of the King* to portray the entrance to the Paths of the Dead. An overnight stay in the small town of Martinborough is highly recommended, where you'll be surrounded by vineyards and olive trees, with some great restaurants where you can sample local specialities. The historic Martinborough Hotel is one of the many fine Victorian buildings you'll see, and is where Viggo Mortensen and other cast stayed during filming.

The drive to Putangirua takes about 45 minutes heading south on Pirinoa Road, turning left towards Cape Palliser and on to the coast, where it's a short drive to the Department of Conservation (DOC) car park, where there is a camping ground.

One of the most spectacular routes to the pinnacles and the filming locations is the walk up the Putangirua streambed. Although it's not a difficult hike, it can take between two and three hours for the return trip, so take some food and drink along with you.

The 'badlands' erosion responsible for the pinnacles occurred as the streambed gradually but steadily exposed layers of gravel to rain and floods — some of the rocks were more resistant, and these were the ones to form the pinnacles or 'hoodoos' as they're also known — the eerie backdrop to Legolas' story of the Army of the Dead.

The view from the bridge at Kaitoke looking towards the Rivendell set.

Kaitoke Regional Park

Kaitoke Regional Park nestles in the foothills of the Tararua Ranges, 12 km north of Upper Hutt. The park covers 2800 ha of mature native forest and is popular for picnics, swimming and walking with the more than 100,000 visitors who come here each year. The temperate rainforest and river made this beautiful area location for Rivendell in *The Lord of the Rings*.

To enter the park, turn off SH2 and travel down Waterworks Road to the Pakuratahi – Hutt Forks car park. Four walks begin near here, and there are many pleasant picnic spots along the rivers and bush fringes. Camping is available on the grassy flats at Kaitoke, where toilets and coin-operated barbecues are also available. The clear pools on the Hutt and Pakuratahi Rivers are ideal for swimming.

The position of Rivendell is sign-posted from the entrance to the park and at the location itself there is an interpretative display showing the construction and final result. Although most exterior shots were digitally rendered, the set constructors built a large set at Kaitoke, including the bedroom where Frodo recovered. The impressive site included scaffolding out into the river along with a man-made river and waterfalls. Over 30 workers began construction in November 1999 and the set was completed in March 2000, with filming undertaken between April and May 2000. During filming there were more than 300 crew on site.

Internet:
www.upperhuttcity.com

From this point, the *Lord of the Rings* set extended out over the river and provided the close up scenes of Frodo recovering and meeting his old friends.

Wellington

Internet:
www.wellingtonnz.com

For splendid views of Wellington, take the Kelburn cable car from downtown to the Botanic Gardens. Dating from 1902 when the cable car was introduced to provide a means of conveyance to the farm 'at the top of the hill', it remains popular with tourists and commuters.

Spend a day visiting some famous and interesting sights, using the free brochures from the local I-Site visitor centre, which will introduce you to the major attractions accessible on foot within the downtown area.

The Museum of New Zealand, Te Papa Tongarewa, on Cable Street is renowned for an exciting modern approach, featuring a number of 'hands-on' exhibitions. Admission is free but charges apply to some exhibitions.

Nearby at 10 Kent Terrace is the Embassy, venue for the World Première of *The Return of the King* in 2003 and the Australasian Première of *King Kong*. Opposite is the newly unveiled salute to Wellington filmmaking — The Tripod.

Walking down Courtenay Place to Lambton Quay you'll pass many restaurants favoured by the stars visiting 'Wellywood', and the little yellow Mini raced along this street in *Goodbye Pork Pie* as the Pork Pie lads headed towards the railway station. Although they didn't have the time, a pause at Dymocks bookshop on Lambton Quay is recommended — they have a fine selection of film related books and figurines.

Wellington boasts a superior suburban railway system and the hub is Wellington Station. New Zealand's largest public building when it was built in 1937, it accommodated 675 head office railway staff. Today 22,000 passengers walk through the concourse daily to catch 390 suburban trains.

With cooperation from New Zealand Rail, a major scene from **Goodbye Pork Pie** was filmed here as the Mini raced through the building, along the platform and finally came to rest in a passing empty goods carriage, bound for the Picton ferry.

Wellington's wonderful green belt provides an ideal opportunity to escape the buzz of the city, and especially interesting is Mt Victoria, used extensively to portray the Outer Shire in *The Fellowship of the Ring*. It provided the first location in 1999, and began a remarkable journey through Middle-earth for Peter Jackson and his crew. For two years they travelled New Zealand, filming at over 150 locations from Te Anau to Matamata.

Just a five-minute drive from downtown, the easiest way to reach the locations is to follow Alexandra Road, which will eventually take you to the summit. It's worth the drive to this point to obtain a panoramic vista of the city. As the road climbs there are a number of parking areas, so watch for one on your left about halfway up, in the apex of a sweeping right-hand turn.

The first major building to incorporate earthquake resistance, the Wellington Railway Station is constructed of 1.75 million bricks and 1500 tonnes of granite and marble.

Feeling hungry — then head for Courtney Place. Several cafés and restaurants here were popular with cast and crew of *The Lord of the Rings Trilogy*.

Made by Weta Workshops, the 6.5 m 6 tonne bronze Tripod which honours New Zealand film took 30 craftspeople and seven contractors more than 10,000 hours to construct.

After parking, take the track going downhill on your right. The pine trees on your left featured in the night scene when the Black Riders chased the Hobbits. A little further down is the leafy lane where Frodo warned them to get off the road. A lot of work has been carried out in this area since filming so the bank looks different. Further on is the area where the Hobbits hid from the Nazgûl, under a large tree stump. The plastic stump is long gone, but this area has become a popular spot for **Lord of the Rings** enthusiasts.

Richard Taylor and his partner Tania relate how a Sunday stroll here after the films had been released became very special for a group of overseas fans. As they reached the stump area a number of tourists with *Lord of the Rings Location Guidebooks* were busy searching for the exact place. Looking up and recognising Richard and Tania from their Oscar appearances, the fans were delighted at the perfect timing of the arrival of two directors of Weta Workshop, who were able to confirm the exact spot — and the fans were very impressed, taking some convincing that this wasn't part of the tour!

Above: Seagulls hover against a strong northerly at Evans Bay near Wellington Airport. These rocks were used as part of *King Kong*'s Skull Island with the help of copious amounts of Green Screen.

Far left: The Bouquet Garni Restaurant on Willis Street is dwarfed by its neighbours

Left: Her journeying to Skull Island over, the SS *Venture* sits quietly at the wharf at Miramar.

Below: Wellington is a city that feels like a village. Friendly people, great restaurants and houses downtown all combine to create an ambience unlike any other city in the country.

New Plymouth

Internet:
www.taranaki.co.nz

www.samuraivillagetours.com

Mt Taranaki broods over a layer of cloud in the early morning with Lake Mangamahoe in the foreground.

Dominating the Taranaki region is the 2518 m high Mt Taranaki (Egmont). Maori legend tells of the beautiful Ruapehu, who was married to Taranaki. One day, while her husband was hunting, she was wooed and won by Tongariro. When Taranaki returned he surprised the guilty pair and a titanic battle ensued in which Taranaki was defeated. He retreated towards the west coast, carving out the course of the Whanganui River as he went.

A prosperous region supplying a significant percentage of New Zealand's domestic gas and oil, the many towns encircling Mt Taranaki (Egmont) support the area's highly productive dairy farms. New Plymouth is the largest and has a wonderful selection of shops, restaurants and cafés.

Personal highlights are Pukeiti Rhododendron Garden, featuring one of the world's largest rhododendron collections, and Puke Ariki Heritage, Knowledge and Information Centre (New Plymouth), a state-of-the-art local museum.

Take the Surf Highway, starting in New Plymouth, and drive around Mt Taranaki (Egmont) via Oakura (where Tom Cruise stayed whilst filming *The Last Samurai*), Opunake to Hawera before returning via Stratford to New Plymouth. Surfers visit the Taranaki region from around the world to ride the waves near Oakura and surf in winter beneath a snow-covered mountain.

When *The Last Samurai* was filmed here, a 200-member crew converged on the set at Uruti to create a traditional Japanese Samurai village from the ground up.

The crew cut horizontally into the hillsides and built on multiple levels. Timber was brought in by helicopter; thatch from a nearby valley was cut and hand-tied, and crops planted. Fabric was dyed and fashioned into large flags to identify the village by its Samurai clan name. With the exception of a small number of props and lanterns imported from Japan, every item was made by the crew using local sources.

Production designer Lilly Kilvert designed the village. 'We had a potter's building complete with baking kiln, a weaver's house, a basket maker, and — this being a Samurai village — a swordsmith and a shrine where, among other things, the blades would be blessed. We also had a water wheel and cistern system, since the Japanese had advanced methods of water delivery and irrigation at the time.'

Kilvert attempted to be as true to the era as possible and provided historical authenticity. 'The most difficult thing we had to do was to honour the rules of Japanese architecture while finding ways to make them photographable. In general, I tried to assemble the essential elements and create an authentic feeling of a particular time.'

Weta Workshops produced over 1700 weapons for *The Last Samurai*, including spears, samurai swords, ninja weapons, cavalry swords, guns and 3500 arrows.

About a week before we started shooting, Ed and Marshall and I just walked though the village by ourselves. We wandered around, looking at the details and discussing how they were made, and it was a wonderful afternoon, with the kind of feeling that makes you feel like a kid. We ate sandwiches and talked about the script, and then there was a moment when we all sat there quietly, just looking around. We knew what was ahead of us, and none of us was in a hurry to leave. It was a wonderful, wonderful moment.

Tom Cruise

"Recreating period Japan by building an entire village on the top of a mountain — it's like going to war. We were moving armies and material on a colossal scale for a company making a movie."
Producer Marshall Herskovitz

Different sorts of troops prepare for battle now that sport has returned to Pukekura Park.

"I saw a place on a high plateau that looked like it could be on a mountainside, because it had elevated ground behind. It just looked like the kind of terrain where Samurai warriors would live."

Charlie Harrington (Location Manager)

The crew who found the locations for ***The Last Samurai*** chose three of the most beautiful parts of the region. Starting downtown, drive (or walk) to Pukekura Park. Opened in 1876, this botanical spectacle covers 49 ha of native growth and formal gardens, two lakes, a fernery and display houses. There is also a Japanese Garden complete with Torii Gate, built to celebrate the tenth anniversary of a sister city relationship with Mishima, Japan. At the entrance to the park, the cricket ground was transformed in 2003 into the Japanese Imperial Parade Ground, with the Bellringer Pavilion receiving a palace façade. Filming here took five days over a five-week period and also featured tents, 300 extras, 50 horses and cannons.

Lake Mangamahoe is a 10-minute drive from town on SH3, east towards Stratford. A beautiful scenic park, it has a number of picnic areas and walkways, as well as a mountain-biking area and horse trails, with impressive views of Mt Taranaki (Egmont). The trees surrounding the lake were used to create the dramatic battle in the fog where Captain Aldren is captured.

The location of the main Samurai Village is on private land, but guided tours are available. Taking half a day from New Plymouth, the tour is a wonderful insight into film production and the life of the Samurai. Although most of the buildings have been removed, some remain and their presence, combined with photo boards and models, provide an enthralling tour of a beautiful part of New Zealand.

The rugged bush country around this area also featured in ***Vigil***, where the rain-soaked grey atmosphere that can pervade these mountainous areas was captured so well on film.

On the drive from New Plymouth to Wanganui, pause at Patea. The beach and wharf here were both used in *River Queen*.

Whanganui River

Internet:
www.wanganui.com
www.whanganuiriver.co.nz

The view from the lookout point at the start of the Whanganui River Road.

Ko au te Awa, ko te Awa ko au.
I am the river, the river is me.

The Whanganui River is New Zealand's second longest river. Starting her life high in the melting snows of Mt Tongariro (one of the central volcanic peaks), she loops north to Taumarunui and then meanders 260 km to the Tasman Sea at Wanganui, with the Whanganui River Road from Wanganui to Pipiriki one of the most scenic and historic drives in New Zealand.

Maori used the river for trade and travel into the Central North Island for centuries, and European discovery of the river turned it into one of our major tourist attractions. The introduction of river boats in the late 1800s to carry tourists saw the river dubbed the 'Rhine of the South Pacific'.

The town of Wanganui sits astride the river where she enters the Tasman Sea, and Whanganui Riverboat Centre at 1A Taupo Quay makes an ideal start for river exploration. Here you can visit and travel on the PS *Waimarie*, the only surviving paddle steamer from the 12-strong fleet run by Alexander Hatrick & Co. For 50 years the PS *Waimarie* journeyed between Wanganui and Pipiriki, carrying passengers, mail and freight inland. Sinking at her berth in 1952, she was carefully restored and returned to her life on the river.

Wanganui also marks the initial destination of Gerry, John and Shirl in **Goodbye Pork Pie**. Scenes were filmed close by the river in town as Shirl changed her mind and decided to travel to Wellington.

Ruatiti Domain is one of those untouched places that make an ideal holiday spot under canvas.

For me **River Queen** has been a passion project undertaken over many years — an opportunity to hook into and journey into a unique part of the Maori realm through the eyes of Sarah, our central character — a woman who through circumstance has values very akin to ours. This allows us to perceive how the exchange between the two cultures might have operated at the interface — and even more so: to live and experience it.

In parts of nineteenth century New Zealand rivers were the only highways, and it is along these rivers from the coastline 'into the interior' that our story takes place. The 'interior' was a large tract of dense bush at the heart of New Zealand's central North Island that was almost impenetrable, where few Europeans dared to venture and fewer still returned. Much of the New Zealand terrain has changed since then, forest has given away to farmland and first-growth native bush is hard to find anywhere close to the major cities, where trees have been felled many times over.

For our unit it meant travelling a crew up rivers close to the actual sites where some of the last warrior chiefs had once reigned, to where 'first growth' native bush still existed with all the primeval majesty of ancient forest. This in turn meant we needed a large and mobile crew to get into and service these inland river locations.

Due to the requirements of the financing for the film and Samantha's changing availability, I found myself, of necessity, shooting in the middle of winter. While this had some advantages in terms of the look of the film, it gave us an unexpected challenge as to how we could best limit the number of water scenes and safeguard our actors while still conveying a strong feeling of interaction with the river. Custom-made water protective dry suits were critical, as they could be worn under their costumes, as well as delaying the filming of the river scenes as long a possible, until spring. And even in the most remote locations, surprisingly close to the shooting — only metres away, you would find a heated tent for actors, to help protect them against the elements.

Preparation for the film was essential and the key crew needed to become very familiar with the locations. I gave detailed demonstrations of how I planned to shoot the particular shots I had in mind for every location, showing crew what particular angles we would use and refining it three or four times over with the many preparatory visits we made.

The years of preparation were paying off, with more than two years of liaison with the local Maori tribes, and research into every possible aspect of that period — from medical practice through the making of ammunition, the varying styles of music — Maori and European, and aspects of the two cultures that had been gleaned from hundreds of books and were now in picture form. I now made them available in huge visual folders for the crew — circling those aspects that were more relevant than others.

Vincent Ward

The river was very effectively used by Director Vincent Ward in **River Queen**, and you can either travel the river with a number of tourist operators or drive from Wanganui to Pipiriki and Raetihi. Allow a day to fully explore the area. If you do decide to drive, your first stop should be at the river lookout a few kilometres after turning off SH4. As the road descends you soon reach the river and for the next 50 km she is never far away.

In the 1840s missionaries journeyed upriver to spread the word of God. One of the first to visit the area, Reverend Taylor, named the small villages that sprang up as a reflection of his Classical education. The Maori pronunciations remain, so you'll pass through Atene (Athens), Koroniti (Corinth), Ranana (London) and Hiruharama (Jerusalem). Each of these small villages has its own story to tell, but Jerusalem is one of the most fascinating, founded in 1883 as a Catholic Mission Station when Mother Mary Joseph Aubert arrived to assist the Sisters of St Joseph. Born in the Loire, this remarkable woman studied medicine and served as a nurse in the Crimea before moving to New Zealand. In 1892 she formed a new diocesan congregation, the Daughters of Our Lady of Compassion, and her founding church still stands.

Another famous New Zealander to live here was the poet James K. Baxter. A controversial figure, Baxter shifted here in 1969 to form a community structured around key 'spiritual aspects of Maori communal life'.

The river is left behind at Pipiriki (where a number of tours can be undertaken on the river) and the road climbs steadily to the volcanic plateau.

One of several flourmills built in the 1800s, the Kawana mill has been immaculately restored. Complete with water wheel and interior machinery, the mill and adjacent miller's cottage now bask in the sun, the wheels quiet.

Evidence of the force of the river can be seen here as timber washed down after a heavy rainfall gathers in the lee corners.

Above and left: The diverse architectural forms in the small village of Jerusalem are parts of its charm, as it nestles into the hills surrounding the river that has been its lifeblood for over a century.

Far left: Koroniti Marae is generally open to visitors, but you should be aware there will be times when it is not appropriate.

Below: One of the main locations in *River Queen* — the Ruatiti Domain.

Tongariro

Internet:
www.visitruapehu.com

The Ratana Church at Raetihi. Founded by Tahupotiki Wiremu Ratana in 1918, the Ratana Faith established many churches, combining spiritual and political elements in order to unite the people under God. Ratana died in 1939 but the faith still remains, its symbol a five-pointed star representing the five-fold elements of divinity, resting on an upturned crescent moon with the words 'T.W. Ratana'.

The Central North Island is an area of distinctive geography and contrasting scenery. In the space of an hour you can travel from a peaceful wonderland of rivers, lakes and pastoral greenery to a blasted, tormented landscape of lava and volcanic ash.

Tongariro National Park was New Zealand's first national park and is a world heritage area. The park was created in 1887 when three volcanoes, Ruapehu, Ngauruhoe and Tongariro, were gifted to the people of New Zealand by Ngati Tuwharetoa, the local iwi.

This area was once one of the most active volcanic areas in the world, with Lake Taupo formed as a result of the largest eruption seen in the last 5000 years. The Oranui Eruption, 26,500 years ago, created the shape of the lake, then in 181AD a further explosion produced an eruption column 50 km high with over 30 km of pumice, ash and rock fragments, with the effects of the eruption seen as far away as Europe and China.

The best base to explore this region is Ohakune, where New Zealand's largest production area of carrots owes its existence to the rich volcanic soil. If you're not into sports of the snowy kind, winter isn't the best time to visit, as the town is full of skiers and snowboarders, and accommodation is at a premium.

The cast and crew for *The Lord of the Rings Trilogy* used Ohakune as base for a number of weeks of filming, with many of them staying at the Powderhorn Chateau.

The area used to film part of Ithilien in *The Two Towers* is on the Turoa Ski Field road (also known as the Ohakune Mountain Road Scenic Drive). The local Department of Conservation office has information on a number of walks and tramps leading from the road. As it climbs steadily, the road provides great views of Mt Ruapehu and the rolling hills around Ohakune, before travelling through beautiful beech forest to the Mangawhero Falls.

If you want to see where Sméagol caught his fish in the moonlight, park in the turn-off area and climb down to the riverbed. As you look towards the waterfall itself, the rocky streambed is apparent but for the final film the background hills were replaced by a painting of larger peaks. On the day the scene was shot, there was an unseasonal snowfall. Undeterred, Peter Jackson had the local volunteer fire brigade wash the snow away before actor Andy Serkis put on a heavy-duty wetsuit and swam across the pool — again and again — until Peter was satisfied and Andy resembled a large iceblock.

Just upstream is where Sam and Frodo are seen walking through an open glade with a ruined column in the background. Carefully cross the stream and walk approximately 50 m into a small clearing to find the spot, with trees surrounding an open grassed area.

In summer the water looks inviting enough, but it belies the cold Andy Serkis endured as he swam looking for fish.

Just above the Mangawhero Falls, looking across stream to where various ruins were placed to represent the declining power of Gondor in Ithilien in *The Two Towers*.

A wonderful day trip can be undertaken from Ohakune to Whakapapa, visiting locations from six different films. Situated 15 km from Ohakune is the small town of Raetihi, tucked into a valley between the Whanganui and Tongariro National Parks. Founded in 1893, its only access was by river until 1917 when both the road and the railway reached their long tentacles into the region.

Today many of the charming buildings from the town's historic past remain, and it became the ideal location for the American hillbilly town in **Without a Paddle**. For the filming, all the road signs in town were reversed to reflect the different traffic regulations in the US, the street layout changed and a number of American vehicles cruised through town on 'the wrong side of the road' as our heroes entered.

Nearby is the beautiful Ruatiti Domain. Travel left off SH2, 1 km past Raetihi and then a further 20 km on a mostly sealed road that can be narrow in places, but the river views are worth every turn in the road. Here a number of scenes from **River Queen** were filmed where the Ruatiti River and Manganui-O-Te Ao Stream converge. The camping ground here is an idyllic spot to spend a few days, lying beside the stream listening to the summer cicadas before taking a dip in the stream.

Returning to SH2 the road runs almost straight to Horopito, the home of **Smash Palace**. This can be visited on your return journey, so for now continue under the Makatote Viaduct. Spanning the Makatote River at a height of 78.6 m and length of 262 m, this steel railway bridge was completed in 1908 and is the third highest in the country. In **Goodbye Pork Pie** there is a memorable scene of the Mini being chased under this bridge by a member of the local constabulary.

At National Park, turn right for The Chateau and Mordor.

The railway at Raurimu where Al Shaw paused as the train raced past on another track. An engineering masterpiece, the Raurimu Spiral begins here as it raises the North Island Main Trunk over 213 m in 11 km via a series of circles and tunnels.

Home to the oldest theatre in the southern hemisphere, Raetihi is a unique example of a pioneering timber town.

At the foot of Mt Ruapehu lies The Grand Chateau, one of this country's most iconic hotels. Built in the 1920s, it features huge floor-to-ceiling windows which make the most of the outstanding views. The Chateau's nearest neighbour, Mt Ruapehu, at 2796 m is the highest peak in the North Island, and one with an explosive history. Eruptions late last century spread ash as far south as Wellington, and spectacular lahars of black mud scarred the normally pristine slopes. The simmering crater is strongly acidic, and occasionally mud and rock are thrown down the mountainside. Part of a volcanic chain extending into the Pacific, extensive seismic measuring equipment provide an early warning system for the surrounding area.

The *Lord of the Rings* team stayed here for a number of weeks, using the conference room as their headquarters. In winter, Whakapapa Ski Field is a playground for skiers who enjoy the après-ski lifestyle. In other seasons it is transformed into an area of mountainous volcanic rock.

To visit the area used to portray the battle marking the end of the Second Age of Middle-earth, drive to Iwikau Village, 15 minutes up the slope from The Grand Chateau. The location is easily accessible, but strong walking shoes or boots are recommended. All around you the twisted landscape of Mordor comes alive in the blasted volcanic rock, steep bluffs and ash-darkened slopes.

The daylight express between Auckland and Wellington crosses the Makatote Viaduct.

From the main building, head north around the learners' ski slope and towards Pinnacle Ridge. Just before you climb the ridge, walk slightly downhill and along the ridge to a viewpoint overlooking a tumbled area with steep escarpments. The slopes and nearby car park were used to film Orcs (played by serving members of the New Zealand Army, stationed nearby at Waiouru) attacking the alliance of Elves and Men. The vast hordes seen in the movie were added by the special-effects team at Weta Studios. As the exposed summer slopes had many vulnerable mountain plants, special care was undertaken during filming with acres of carpet laid to protect soil and vegetation.

A Hillman Super Minx shows a new form of power under the bonnet.

The rocky outcrop known as Meads Wall beside Pinnacle Ridge was used in *The Two Towers* when Frodo and Sam capture Gollum by pretending to sleep as he stalks them down the rocky face. The special suit Andy Serkis wore during filming provided authentic body movements which were then captured and used to create Gollum at Weta Studios.

The strange volcanic wastes evoke Mordor, particularly when the weather is overcast and dark clouds swirl around the peaks. Close-up scenes of Frodo and Sam's epic trek towards Mount Doom were shot here in this basin, along with the sequence showing them lost in the rocky wasteland of the Emyn Muil.

Returning now to National Park, many parts of *The Navigator* were filmed in this area, and the main road just before reaching the small village was used to film Al Shaw as he raced his car past police in *Smash Palace*.

Most of the latter film was shot at Smash Palace itself, which can be visited on the return trip to Ohakune at Horopito. The car museum there is open five days a week for visitors and a small admission is charged.

As the Main Trunk line neared completion in this part of the Central North Island, a temporary work camp sprang up. Sawmilling began and plans were made for a town, but by the late 1960s little remained except for Horopito Motors. Established by Bill Cole in the 1940s, the garage and repair shop continued to expand. He believed every car that made it to his yard should remain after spare parts had been sold, and by 1981 acres of cars made an ideal location for *Smash Palace*.

It's very easy to spend an hour wandering through them. Early vintage types are barely recognisable amongst smaller English cars of the 1960s, as ferns and moss reclaim their ownership of the land through bonnets and windows. Car shapes not seen for many years are a reminder of holiday trips as a child, while others slowly rust away. One of these is the Valiant that appeared in *Goodbye Pork Pie*.

Opposite above: The Morris Collection including the ubiquitous 'land-crab' of the 1960s.

Opposite below: A 'flax' display of car parts hoist a Morris Marina skyward.

71

Taupo

Internet:
www.laketauponz.com

Above: The mountains of the Central Plateau hide under a cloak of cloud whilst Lake Taupo glistens under the morning sun.

Below: The drive from Tongariro to Taupo is one of dramatic contrasts, from the ashen volcanic plateau to the beautiful Lake Rotoaira, nestled in the bush.

Opposite: The Huka Falls and their approach are an insight into the sheer power of water. As the Waikato squeezes through a narrow granite chasm, the river is suddenly expelled over the falls.

Situated on the shores of our largest lake, Taupo is the commercial centre of the region. Established as a tourist area almost since settlement began in the 1840s, Taupo is ideally situated on the main State Highway with many opportunities to swim and sail on the lake as well as an abundance of adrenaline-inducing activities in the air and on the ground.

The lakes and streams here are world renowned for trout fishing. Over 100 years ago trout were released and now people travel from around the world to fish the lake and its tributary streams. The Tongariro River has over 80,000 trout run through spawning season, and the lake itself sees 160,000 fish caught annually.

Heading northwards from town, you cross the Waikato, the longest river in New Zealand. Here boats are tied up to the shore and willows provide shade for picnickers — however, a few kilometres north of here the river takes a more dramatic form: the Huka Falls.

These are a must-see and can be visited from a small loop road off SH1. Don't expect a precipitous drop — it's the sheer volume of water that's so astounding. As the Waikato River leaves Lake Taupo it is suddenly confined into a narrow 15 m wide rock-bound chasm. For 250 m the river churns its way towards a 10 m cliff into a wide basin creating a roaring mass of water and foam as over 3,000,000 l a second drops into the basin.

Scenes from *Without a Paddle* were filmed at both the falls and the river area. There are a number of walks from the falls as well, and it is quite a dramatic contrast to walk alongside a calm flowing river one minute then cross the bridge over a raging torrent.

Matamata

Internet:
www.matamata-info.com
www.hobbittontours.com

Below: Nestled into the rolling green hills of Matamata is the area Peter Jackson has made famous as the location of Hobbiton in *The Lord of the Rings Trilogy*.

Opposite and overleaf: Arguably the most famous movie set in the world, the impact of the filming of *The Lord of the Rings Trilogy* will be seen in New Zealand for many years to come. Surveys show that over 100,000 people have visited this country since the release of the films, specifically because of their interest in visiting the locations. Restoration work of the hobbit holes has been undertaken to ensure their longevity. Although some were initially removed after filming, Bag End, the home of Bilbo and Frodo Baggins, remains as a monument to the creative genius of Peter Jackson and his team.

The Waikato region of the North Island is one of the richest farming areas in New Zealand, and a district of rolling grassy hills. In 1855 Yorkshireman Josiah Clifton Firth emigrated from England and purchased 56,000 acres of swampy marshland. He had in mind the rich agricultural Fens in his native England, and began large-scale drainage of the marshes, planting in their place vast paddocks of grass and grain. As the years passed hedgerows were planted alongside oaks and elms, and as the railway moved steadily south from Auckland the area prospered. Still a rural service town, Matamata's rich grassland now produces another lucrative crop, as the Waikato has developed into New Zealand's premier racehorse-breeding area.

While private tours are not allowed, guided tours to Hobbiton operate daily, with bookings for the two-hour excursion available at the Visitor Information Centre in town. Middle-earth's Shire was recreated on part of a working sheep farm owned by the Alexander family, whose story you will hear from your tour guide.

You will enter the farm on a road built by the New Zealand Army to give the filmmakers access to the site during filming, and as you climb the brow of a hill the set lies directly ahead of you. On a stroll through Hobbiton, your guide will explain how the set developed and there are plenty of opportunities for photographs. Conveniently situated photo-boards show how the area looked during filming and how the set designers achieved that amazing finished look. The culmination of the tour is a walk up Bagshot Row to Bag End and the opportunity to stand outside the most famous hobbit hole in Middle-earth.

I am one of three brothers, along with my father, involved in the sheep and beef farm where 'Hobbiton' was filmed for **The Lord of the Rings Trilogy** directed by Peter Jackson. Peter's location scout first saw the property from the air where they were attracted by the green lush rolling countryside, lake and the now famous 'party tree'.

While the whole movie experience is hard to describe, I can say it has changed my life forever. Our first thoughts after being approached were to wonder what we were letting ourselves in for. We took our time (six months) in talking over what was going to be involved, which was probably, to this day, the best thing we did as there haven't really been any surprises, except the enormity of the success of the films and now the tourist venture, which has turned out to be much bigger than we ever anticipated.

When Ian Brodie asked me what it's like to have a world-famous movie set on your land, all I could say is that it has been a wonderful experience and opportunity. The best part is the people you meet from many different parts of the world, all with different experiences and cultures to share; it has been a privilege and opened doors to myself and our staff.

We've now travelled to different parts of the world and within New Zealand we would otherwise never have visited. I have met some wonderful people, all with individual stories to tell, from set builders, TV personalities, business people, celebrities through to people like Ian Brodie and his wife Dianne. Along the way I've learnt and experienced a lot about another two new industries — film and tourism.

From the first location negotiations starting back in September 1998, right through to our tourist attraction here today, it is an experience that is forever challenging, as you are continually searching for ideas for improvement or enhancement. Like any rewarding experience it's not all plain sailing, and comes at a cost in the sense of your time for other interests and family.

If I have one regret, it's that I didn't take enough time to take stock of what was actually happening at the time; what was actually done, the transformation of a paddock and the attention to detail of the set builders and art directors; they demanded perfection and achieved this wonderful, surreal place we are now privileged to share with others.

Russell Alexander

South Island locations

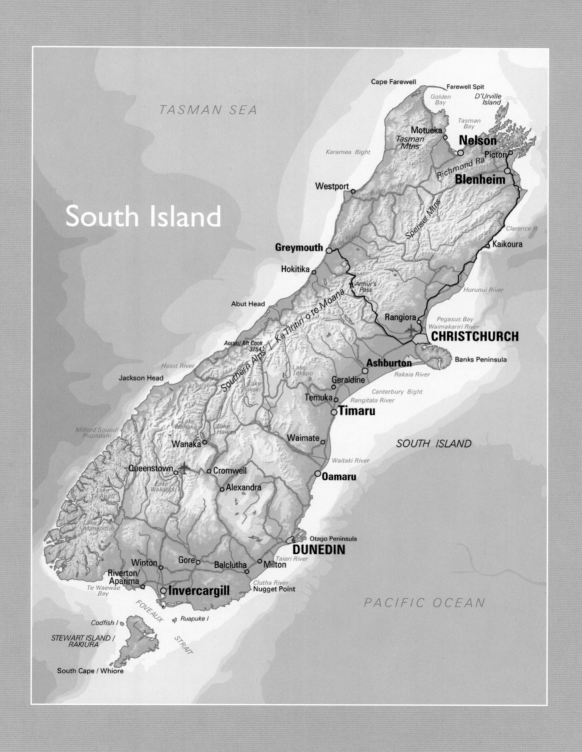

TASMAN SEA

Cape Farewell Farewell Spit
Golden   D'Urville
Bay   Island

Tasman
Bay

Motueka
Tasman   Nelson
Mtns
Karamea Bight   Picton

Richmond Ra
Westport   Blenheim
Buller River

South Island   *Spenser Mtns*
Greymouth   Clarence R
Hokitika   Kaikoura

Arthur's   *Hurunui River*
Pass
Abut Head   Rangiora   *Pegasus Bay*
Waimakariri River

Aoraki/Mt Cook *Ka Tiritiri o te Moana*   CHRISTCHURCH
37541
Haast River   Ashburton   Banks Peninsula
Jackson Head   *Lake*   Geraldine   *Rakaia River*
Tekapo
Lake   Temuka   *Canterbury Bight*
Pukaki   Timaru   *Rangitata River*

Milford Sound/   *Lake*   Waimate
Piopiotahi   *Wanaka*   *Lake*
Wanaka *Hawea*   *Waitaki River*   SOUTH ISLAND

Queenstown   Cromwell   Oamaru
Lake
Te Anau *Lake*   Alexandra
Wakatipu

Lake   Otago Peninsula
Manapouri   DUNEDIN
Winton   Gore   Balclutha Milton *Taieri River*
Riverton/   *Clutha River*
Aparima   Nugget Point
Te Waewae Invercargill
Bay   *FOVEAUX*   PACIFIC OCEAN
Codfish I   Ruapuke I
STEWART ISLAND /   *STRAIT*
RAKIURA

South Cape / Whiore

Autumn colours, Central Otago,

Mountains near Wanaka

Fishing boats at Westport.

The West Coast of the South Island is a region of abundant native bush, deep blue lakes, clear streams and snow-capped peaks. Receiving much more rainfall than its eastern neighbour, the consequent growth has resulted in a region of luxuriant trees and bush.

Known by New Zealanders simply as 'The Coast', this narrow province sandwiched between the Southern Alps and the Tasman Sea had its fair share of lawlessness during the mid-1800s when miners laboured to recover rich alluvial gold from its many rivers.

Today tourism is a major industry and the West Coast Road which stretches over 400 km from Karamea in the north to Haast in the south is a well-travelled tourist route.

With a population of 6000, the town of Westport sits where the Buller River meets the Tasman Sea, and it was here that **Perfect Strangers** began and ended.

A day can easily be spent exploring the locations between Westport and Punakaiki (a 40-minute drive south on SH6). First stop should be Tauranga Bay near Cape Foulwind; it was here that Melanie and The Man dance around the bonfire. Return to SH6 via Wilson's Lead Road, travel south to Charleston and then right to Constant Bay. It was through this tiny entrance from the roaring Tasman that both the *Marauder* and *Dauntless* sailed to reach the beach. They weren't the first to undertake this hazardous journey — in 1866 Captain Charles Bonner sailed the *Constant* into the bay to provide much needed supplies to the waiting miners. The local tavern, and its café, at Charleston has many photos detailing the colourful history of the area and makes a great refreshment stop along the way.

West Coast

Internet:
www.west-coast.co.nz

Limestone formations near Punakaiki have been formed over millions of years as sea, wind and rain have eroded the soft layers to leave the harder structure exposed.

The narrow inlet at Constant Bay looks calm on a nice day, but when the sea awakens it becomes one of the most treacherous harbour entrances in New Zealand.

Above: The coal mine in the skies. Coal remains as the buildings slowly rust under the elements. Remnants of a colourful past have created a ghost town that rivals any in the world.

Right: From this angle the height of Denniston is dramatically apparent. The incline dropped over the cliff face on its controlled race to the station below.

Continue southwards now to Meybille Bay, the idyllic location used in the film. This small crib (in southern vernacular) appeared to be on a remote island, but in reality it's one of many with waves lapping their doors, surrounded by sand and bush with the roaring sea constantly echoing through their rooms.

The real life *Perfect Strangers* beach is almost inaccessible by foot. Irimahuwheri Bay is best viewed from the high lookout point (sign-posted past Meybille Bay).

One of the major tourist attractions of the Coast is a further 10-minute drive away —the stacked pancake rocks at Punakaiki.

Whilst in Westport another must-see is the deserted mining town of Denniston, high in the hills inland from Waimangaroa and only 15 km north of Westport.

In 1873 coal was discovered on the Mt Rochfort Plateau. The problem was the area's extreme location — how to get the coal down from 520 metres above sea level. In 1879 an ingenious railway incline was developed. Until it closed in 1967, a total of 13 million tonnes of coal was carried down the escarpment to Waimangaroa and then on to the waiting ships at Westport.

Now the area is a ghost town. The drive up the narrow winding road is nothing compared to the original means of access — riding empty wagons — but the view from the top is superb. Invariably the clouds swirl around this ghost town of deserted diggings, adding to its sense of isolation.

The combination of sea, sand and bush on West Coast beaches are a delight, but when mixed in with quiet isolation and stirred with a gentle breeze they create a fantastic holiday escape.

I grew up in a small town participatory culture and because of the geographic isolation, everyone gets good at a lot of things — makes for a very resourceful community. I hope they never lose that. The place is booming now, and they are celebrating their history and saving more old buildings than ever before. I miss that pounding sea and those big black hills, but I get back there a bit because the whanau is there.

The place is not merely a backdrop but rather more like a fourth character. It moans, it gleams, it imposes itself on every scene. That's because some of Melanie's conflict comes from being stuck in a threatening and alien environment from which she cannot escape. I was very lucky to have Alun Bollinger as cinematographer because he knows the place even better than I do. We were filming over the road from his home. It's a psychological and spiritual place. Our turangawaewae, so to speak. I believe film captures the spirit of things along with the more obvious things like the light and the dark.

Gaylene Preston, Director, *Perfect Strangers* (Salient)

One of the key visual elements in **Perfect Strangers** is the landscape. We chose a hut location with views out the windows that it was important to make use of. That's always a challenge, getting exteriors to read when shooting location interiors. Bindy Crayford (my gaffer) and her team devised a rig that hung out from the roof of the hut and could be raised and lowered without too much hooha, so we could push light into the hut from outside the windows but keep the rig out of shot. And the art department gave us a couple of skylights in the roof that we got good use out of. In fact, the lighting department spent quite a lot of their time up on the roof of that hut, as it was the only clear flat space on or around the location — they reckoned they got the best views from up there.

Alun Bollinger, Cine Photographer, *Perfect Strangers* (On Film)

The *Cordyline* (cabbage tree) is a familiar sight throughout New Zealand. The centre leaves were eaten as a substitute for cabbage by early European settlers — hence the rather unusual name.

Above: The slender Dorothy Falls (63.1 m) are just a short walk from the road that circles Lake Kaniere.

Below: Revington's Hotel is a survivor from the gold field days when hotels sprouted from every corner to extract hard-earned money from the miners and satiate their thirst.

Right: Recently unveiled, the memorial to commemorate the four police officers and three civilians killed by Graham in 1941 was crafted by retired police officer, Barry Thomson. Weighing 7.1 tonne, the granite monument features a viewing hole at its centre, aligned towards where the Graham house stood and the murders took place.

Greymouth, the largest town on the West Coast is 105 km south of Westport. Settled by the Europeans in 1863, gold was soon discovered and the town boomed as settlers moved in to make their fortune. In the centre of town on Tainui Street is Revington's Historic Hotel. Built in 1876, it stands as a proud reminder of the many hotels that once graced this town. Like Queen Elizabeth, who visited in 1954, you can stay here and walk across the threshold for a drink, where Melanie met The Man in *Perfect Strangers*, then take a stroll down to the Fisherman's Wharf, where the pair left civilisation behind.

Travelling south, the town of Hokitika is only a 20-minute drive away. En route two bridges are crossed that are now something of an oddity — the rail and road combine on one track to span the river. Founded on gold, Hokitika is the gateway to the South Westland World Heritage National Park. A number of shops sell pounamu — the prized greenstone of the Maori, known to the rest of world as jade.

A 2-hour return drive inland from Hokitika is recommended to visit Lake Kaniere and the quiet rural village of Kowhitirangi. Nestled under the Southern Alps, its peaceful green pastures belie the bloody events that happened here in 1941. This area was the location used in the 1981 film *Bad Blood* to portray the killings and subsequent manhunt of Stanley Graham, where a memorial remembers those killed in New Zealand's first mass murder.

Returning to the small settlement of Kokatahi, continue now to Lake Kaniere. This blue gem settles amongst the green it frequently mirrors. An ideal picnic spot, it is a favourite local summer haunt for swimming and boating.

Travelling south on SH6, the journey from Hokitika to Haast is a delight. Stunning lakes reflect the intense green of the verdant native bush, and tumbling rivers reach for the sea from the snow-capped peaks of the Southern Alps that tower above on your left.

The small locality of Harihari is reached 79 km south of Hokitika. There is a small café shop on the main street, so pause for a tea, coffee or ice-cream. Gerry and John did in their Mini, serving the visiting family of holidaymakers at the same time in *Goodbye Pork Pie*. A further 70 km southward will bring you to Franz Josef Glacier.

When Director Peter Jackson needed a location to portray the Lighting of the Beacons in *The Lord of the Rings — The Return of the King*, he chose a mountain-top near Queenstown. However, with draught conditions and a total fire ban when filming was due to start, he had to change his plans. After searching the West Coast he settled on Mt Gunn at Franz Josef, which provided some of the trilogy's most stunning aerial shots as peak after peak blazed as the fiery beacons passed Gandalf's message across Middle-earth.

Take the glacier access road through the bush for wonderful views and the unusual sight of a glacier plunging to the bush-line — something rarely seen outside polar regions.

The best view of Mt Gunn is by helicopter or aeroplane, and there are a number of scenic flight operators based in the village. In addition to views of the location, you will have the opportunity to view Mt Aoraki (Cook) and some flights offer a landing on the glacier.

Fox Glacier is a further 25 km away and the road continues south, cutting a swathe through the bush to the coastal village of Haast. The local DOC Information Centre has good interpretive displays about the region, where the nearby swamp was used as a reference for The Dead Marshes in *The Lord of the Rings — The Two Towers*.

The café on the main street of Harihari still beckons customers for tea and cakes as it did in the 1970s in *Goodbye Pork Pie*.

Lake Ianthe is just one of the lake-jewels between Greymouth and Haast.

Wanaka

Internet:
www.lakewanaka.co.nz

The setting sun lights the golden tussock hills surrounding Lake Hawea. The road from Haast and Makarora traverses the left-hand side of the lake.

Wanaka is reached via the 563.9 m Haast Pass. After leaving Makarora, the road clings to the cliffs with dramatic views of the lake, which made the perfect place for a spectacular car chase in *Goodbye Pork Pie*.

Crossing the narrow 'Neck' from Lake Wanaka takes you to Lake Hawea, where the Mini finally won the race when the police Holden crashed into the undergrowth on the side of the lake.

The glacial Lake Hawea is 30 km long and 390 m deep with excellent fishing from the shores or by boat. The small village of Hawea nestles at the southerly end and features a hotel with adjoining restaurant. A popular place for locals and tourists, the view from the balcony up the lake must be one of the finest in the world.

A further 15-minute drive will take you to Lake Wanaka. Now one of the fastest-growing areas in New Zealand, Lake Wanaka makes for a pleasant stopover. An interesting attraction is Stuart Landsboroughs Puzzling World & Great Maze. Among its many attractions is a forced-perspective room which allows you to interactively experience how some of the point-of-view scenes were filmed in *The Lord of the Rings Trilogy*.

Once you arrive in Wanaka, stop at the waterfront, where the Alps at the end of the lake were used as a backdrop when Gandalf flew to Rohan with Gwaihir, after his rescue from Orthanc. Wanaka Airport is well worth a stop. As well as the airworthy fighter aircraft at the NZ Fighter Pilots Museum, you can follow Orlando Bloom's footsteps and take a tandem skydive, take a *The Lord of the Rings Trilogy* location flight with Wanaka Flightseeing and attempt to emulate Legolas' archery expertise at Have A Shot.

Take the road marked Glendhu Bay and Treble Cone Ski Field and after approximately 15 km you'll pass Glendhu Bay on your right. Continue towards Treble Cone and just before the ski-field turn-off you will have a view of one of the locations used in *Lord of the Rings*. A dramatic ruin was digitally imposed on the large brown hill on your right and used in an aerial sequence, as the Fellowship headed south from Rivendell in *The Fellowship of the Ring*.

Return to Wanaka then take SH89 to Queenstown. The road soon starts to climb through the Cardrona Valley and after a 20-minute drive you'll pass the Cardrona Ski Field entrance on your right. A very popular winter ski-field for novice and expert alike, many scenes were taken here for *Willow*.

The road continues to climb steadily towards the 1119.7 m Crown Range summit where you can park and explore.

A North American P-51D Mustang airborne over the Clutha River near Wanaka. The hills in the centre far background appeared in *The Fellowship of the Ring* as Arwen raced to the Ford with Frodo.

When the nor'west Fohn wind blows, the sky becomes alive with colour and form.

The Kawarau River rushes past Chard Farm Vineyard and towards the old suspension bridge, now locally just called Bungy Bridge. Here the Pillars of the Argonath were digitally inserted.

The view is a treat for **Lord of the Rings** fans. To the left are the locations used for the River Anduin and the Pillars of the Argonath, and high in the hills (straight ahead) is the area used to depict Dimrill Dale. If you travel downhill another kilometre and make another stop, to your right is the location of the Ford of Bruinen and in the far distance the site used for Amon Hen nestles on the shore of the movie's Nen Hithoel. This area was also used for publicity stills of the Fellowship as they headed south in the rough country of Eregion.

The road continues in a series of tight curves, before reaching a shelf of rich farmland with brown hills frowning on the right. There is another steep, downward spiral and six hairpin turns to negotiate to reach the valley floor. Turn left for a short drive to the location of the Pillars of the Kings and a glass of fine Central Otago wine.

Another 5 km on and you'll cross the Kawarau River, where you'll find the headquarters of A. J. Hackett Bungy. Bungy jumping originated as a religious ritual in Vanuatu, and with the help of Kiwi A.J. Hackett and speed-skier, Henry Van Asch, has since become a world-wide adventure sport. The pair came up with the idea of jumping from a great height attached to an elastic bungy cord after watching videos of experiments by the Oxford University Dangerous Sports Club. Hackett's jump from the Eiffel Tower in 1987 created huge interest, and in November 1988 the historic Kawarau Suspension Bridge became the world's first 'bungy bridge'. There are now six bungy sites in the Queenstown area, including the 134-m high Nevis Highwire.

Immediately opposite A. J. Hackett's is the entrance road to Chard Farm Vineyard and a spectacular view of where The Pillars of the Kings were computer-generated into each side of the river in *The Fellowship of the Ring*.

Continuing along this short road brings you to Chard Farm, one of the first commercial vineyards in the Southern Lakes District. Since the vineyard's establishment in 1987, the area has become one of New Zealand's most distinctive wine regions. Perched on the southern edge of the grape-growing world, it's where you'll find New Zealand's highest vineyard above sea level and furthest vineyard from the sea. Warm dry summers, cool autumns and cold winters, with relatively low humidity, and a large 'day-night' temperature range sealing in flavours in white wines and encouraging colour in Pinot Noir, these conditions have contributed to the success enjoyed by local wines. While cellar-door sales at Chard Farm are available seven days from 10 a.m. to 5 p.m., winery tours are by appointment.

Closer to Cromwell is Gibbston Valley Wines, with a wine cave dug deep into the Central Otago schist. With an excellent restaurant and nearby cheese factory, daily tours are available between 10 a.m. and 4 p.m. Each tour culminates in the cave, where the vineyard's wines can be enjoyed in unique surroundings.

The Central Otago region is justifiably proud of its fruit and wine. Pinot grapes ripen at Mt Difficulty whilst apples in an orchard across the road are ready for picking.

Queenstown

Internet:
www.queenstown-nz.co.nz

One of this country's best known and most popular tourist destinations, Queenstown lies in a beautiful alpine valley alongside Lake Wakatipu.

Maori legend tells of an evil tipua (demon) who seized a beautiful girl. While the demon slept, her faithful lover rescued her, setting fire to her captor. The demon woke screaming as flames consumed him, and he drew his knees up in agony. As his body fat melted, it fanned the flames, and as he writhed he dug a huge chasm in the earth. Rain and snow finally extinguished the flames, but by then the demon had been destroyed and the lovers were safe. As time passed, it became apparent his heart had survived, deep in the lake that now bears the outline of his body, it's beating measured by the rise and fall of the lake.

William Gilbert Rees and Nicholas von Tunzelmann were the first Europeans to settle in the area, after cutting their way through the thorny undergrowth with a herd of sheep. They settled their flock near Lake Wakatipu, not realising their peaceful existence would last only until William Fox discovered gold in the Arrow River. Queenstown became the major service centre supplying the thousands of miners and the population exploded.

Now known as The Adventure Capital of New Zealand, tourism is the new 'gold mine' and visitors from around the world have taken the place of the miners — over one million each year. There are too many tourist activities to list here, but it's safe to say there is something for every taste and age.

For many, a highlight is a ride on the grand old lady of the lake. Well over 90 years old and still going strong, the venerable steamer SS *Earnslaw* was built in 1912. Just over 50 m in length and with a beam of 7.3 m, the stately old girl offers a number of excursions on Lake Wakatipu, with the cruise to Walter Peak offering distant views of Closeburn, the location for Amon Hen in ***The Fellowship of the Ring***.

The gondola ride on Bob's Peak, one of the world's steepest cableways, offers a breathtaking view. Rising some 446 m over a distance of 731 m, the fully licensed restaurant at the top provides one of the most romantic dinner venues possible.

While snow-covered winter streets excite skiers, Queenstown can be enjoyed all year round, with summer temperatures reaching over 30° Celsius.

Rugged country near Queenstown.

Arrowtown

Nowhere are the colours of autumn more spectacular than in Arrowtown. The last vestiges of colour cling to the branches as wintry frosts encroach.

Situated at Wilcox Green, a short walk from Arrowtown are The Gladden Fields that appeared in *The Fellowship of the Ring*.

In 1862 William Fox discovered one of the world's richest alluvial gold-bearing areas in Arrowtown, a scenic 20-minute drive from Queenstown, and more than 7000 Europeans and Chinese came to try their luck in the Arrow and Shotover Rivers. The excellent Lakes District Centennial Museum situated on the narrow one-way main street provides a wealth of information, including the infamous and fascinating characters who worked the gold fields.

If you can, visit in autumn, when the tree-lined main street is carpeted in red and gold, and smoke from the chimneys of the original miners' cottages weaves in and out of shafts of sunlight. Sombre pines on the nearby hills are interplanted with larches, which blaze into golden pools of colour in the crisp, early morning air. Many of Arrowtown's shops and galleries feature local artists and craftspeople, so take your time to browse and don't forget your camera.

A short walk from the main street are a number of restored Chinese miners' cottages, and you can still fossick for gold, as stores on the main street hire out pans. Not far away the world-famous Millbrook Resort features luxurious accommodation and restaurants surrounded by a par-72 world championship golf course, designed by Sir Bob Charles, New Zealand's renowned master golfer.

The dramatic scene from *The Fellowship of the Ring* which featured Frodo and Arwen's flight to the Ford at Bruinen was filmed minutes from the centre of the village on the Arrow River, an easy walk from the car park behind the main street. To reach the exact spot, wade upstream in the ankle deep water for some 200 m, which will place you in the direction the Nazgûl charged as Arwen ferried Frodo across the river. The path the Nazgûl took is clearly visible on your left.

During the three days spent here, locals lined the riverbank to watch filming and the Saffron Restaurant was one of the cast's favourite dinner locations.

As you return to Queenstown, the Coronet Peak ski area is on your right, with an sealed access road further on, which offers an imposing view of the Wakatipu Basin from the car park, 1188 m above sea level.

With five ski-fields catering for all levels of ability situated within 90-minutes' drive of Queenstown, it's not surprising that skiing and snowboarding are popular. Every year international visitors descend on the Southern Lakes Region to enjoy the spectacular winter conditions.

The Coronet Peak road also provides access to Skippers Canyon, where you

can stop and admire the view at the turn-off. Local 4WD operator Nomad Safaris offer a number of specialist Lord of the Rings Tours into the canyon. Notoriously tortuous in places, the Skippers Road is closed to rental cars and can be hazardous for drivers not experienced in these sorts of conditions.

At its peak, Skippers was the most prolific of the local gold fields, with each square foot reputed to hold an ounce of gold. A guided tour into the canyon and down to the river takes you through steep valley walls, winding road, stark brown hills and contrasting snow-covered peaks. About 12 km into the gorge, close by the original bridge, was the area used in *The Fellowship of the Ring* as the Ford of Bruinen in flood.

Heading further on towards Queenstown, you will pass historic Gantleys Restaurant on your left, a favourite of cast and crew, and the Quality Resort Alpine Lodge which was used for many interior shots during wet weather.

The Ford of Bruinen in Skippers Canyon.

95

Deer Park Heights

Deer Park Heights is an 800 m conical hill located at Kelvin Heights, off the main road to Te Anau and about 20 minutes' drive from Queenstown.

Its summit is laced with a number of walkways, leading to many locations from *The Lord of the Rings* films, all with panoramic views, and tame llamas, deer, goats and bison. To the north, the river used for the River Anduin can be seen flowing towards the Pillars of the Kings. The hillside was used for locations in all three *Lord of the Rings* films, and all locations from the three films are clearly marked. As well as *The Lord of the Rings Trilogy* locations, there's an unusual sight at the top of the hill — part of a Korean prison set left from the 1986 film *The Rescue*.

About 500 m south of the car park you'll see a small mountain tarn used to film a short sequence of Gandalf's journey to Minas Tirith on the West Road to Gondor, and the edge of the larger tarn near the top car park was used to film the refugees from Rohan fleeing to Edoras after the destruction of their village.

Further down the hill is another small tarn where Gimli was thrown from his runaway horse, and if you carry on another 500 m towards the radio towers you'll come across a walking trail to the cliff face Aragorn disappeared over in the dramatic clash between the Warg-riding Orcs and the Riders of Rohan in *The Two Towers*. But instead of the sheer fall you'd expect from the movie, you'll see a grassy slope. Aragorn's awakening by the water was filmed in Wellington.

Above: Looking across Lake Wakatipu towards Cecil Peak. Deer Park Heights was one of the most frequently used locations in *The Lord of the Rings*.

Below: The grassy slope where Wargs charged in *The Two Towers*.

Below right: The view from the lookout atop Deer Park Heights. The Kawarau River flows towards the Pillars of the Kings.

The Road to Glenorchy

The scenic drive to Glenorchy follows Lake Wakatipu for 45 km, climbing high bluffs with extended views of the lake and mountains, and passing through secluded bays where pine trees cover the lower slopes, with some well-maintained walkways. Have your fishing rod handy: brown and rainbow trout cruise close to the shore — Viggo Mortensen spent a lot of time fly-fishing here, when he wasn't being Aragorn, although you will need to organise a fishing licence first.

Continue beyond Closeburn for 4 km and you'll come to Twelve Mile Delta, an area of regenerating native bush complete with a mountain stream. Here you'll also find a large managed camping area, and a number of walks and mountain-bike tracks will take you into Ithilien. A short drive from Queenstown, it's an ideal camping or picnic spot, totally removed from civilisation. Two areas were used here to portray Ithilien, one on the riverbed and the other on the higher plateau. The riverbed scenes shot here for *The Two Towers* were spectacular and it was here that Sam saw the legendary Oliphants. To reach this location, go down to the river and walk towards Lake Wakatipu.

On your right is the bank where Frodo, Sam and Sméagol lay in hiding to watch the battle between the fierce warriors of Harad and the Rangers of Gondor. If you return to the western end of the river, a walking track will take you to their cliff-top hiding space and the cover where Sam and Sméagol discussed the best way to eat rabbit.

Follow the track to a footbridge spanning a deep chasm over Twelve Mile Stream. About 10 minutes' walk along the track and you'll be where Sméagol caught the coneys. You can also walk through the undergrowth to the cliff edge where the trio watched the battle. There is a dangerous overhang, so don't try to get too close to the edge. In the spring and summer, herbs and wildflowers bloom on beside the track and it's not hard to see why Peter Jackson chose to film Ithilien here, where wildflowers struggle against tough, spiky matagouri bushes. It's the perfect evocation of Sauron's evil pall spreading through Middle-earth. The track continues up to the next plateau with superb views of lake and mountains.

Glenorchy

As you leave the village going north, take the road marked Paradise, passing on your left a beautiful private home, that was once the Arcadia Guesthouse.

Internet:
www.glenorchy.com

Continuing on, the open river flats give way to patches of native beech forest. New Zealand beech contains a number of different sub-species, so while red beech flourishes in frost-free areas, silver beech happily occupies areas covered by winter snow. While some say Paradise was named because of its beauty and others that it's for the wild Paradise Ducks that live here, everyone can agree that it is a spectacular location.

Dan's Paddock, where Gandalf rode up to Isengard in *The Fellowship of the Ring* is 26 km from Glenorchy, and the area up on your right (where paddock and forest meet) was where they filmed his ride.

The high peak of Mt Earnslaw towering over the paddock was used to portray part of The Misty Mountains in the opening of *The Two Towers*, and a number of scenes were filmed here for *Vertical Limit*.

Travel another 2 km through more beautiful forest and open paddocks and, just after leaving a clearing to enter a forest glade, stop at the edge of the forest, which was used to portray the Fellowship entering Lothlórien in *The Fellowship of the Ring*.

Past this point the going gets rough and the best way to see this area is on one of the excursions operated by Dart River Safaris and Dart Stables. Many of the guides worked on *The Lord of the Rings* films and have some interesting experiences to relate.

Take the Routeburn Track Road to the best view of the location where Weta Studios digitally added Isengard as it nestled into Nan Curunír (the Wizard's Vale) with the mighty peak of Methedras towering over the valley. Departing Glenorchy, initially take the Glenorchy–Paradise Road before turning left onto the road marked Kinloch and Routeburn. After crossing the Dart River, turn immediately right and travel 2 km. The best view is some 100 m past the Scott Creek crossing.

Initially, a helicopter with large 'Spacecam' camera mounted underneath was flown in precise circles around the area, gathering landscape images. A miniature Orthanc was added and bush-covered hills filmed on the West Coast added. Finally the Dart River was removed and hundreds of hours of digital work later Middle-earth was on film.

The ridge of Mt Earnslaw that appeared in the opening sequence of *The Two Towers*.

99

Te Anau

Internet:
www.fiordland.org.nz

Te Anau sits beside one of the most beautiful of New Zealand's many spectacular lakes. For the consummate Tolkien experience, stand on the lakefront and follow the brooding bush-covered foothills skywards to towering peaks, and you'll see for yourself why Peter Jackson chose to film the mountainous realms of Middle-earth here.

As well as being the gateway to Fiordland National Park, Lake Te Anau is the second largest lake in New Zealand, covering 43,200 ha and over 417 m in depth. To do the area justice, you'll need at least three days for some spectacular journeys to Milford Sound, Doubtful Sound and the Te Ana-au Caves.

New Zealand's most accessible fiord, each year Milford Sound sees thousands of tourists. The fly/drive option into the area is a popular choice, with fabulous aerial views of the world-renowned Milford Track, Sutherland Falls (one of the world's highest at 580.3 m) and the Sound itself. After landing at the small airfield, a number of cruise options out to the open sea are available. The view from the mouth of the fiord is stunning, with the return by coach equally impressive, stopping at the Chasm, where the Cleddau River has carved its way through solid rock, and the Homer Tunnel.

A visit to the Redcliff Bar & Café, frequented by *The Lord of the Rings* stars during filming, is highly recommended. One evening their meal coincided with the local poetry-reading session. After various recitations a deep voice

resounded, reciting a Shakespearian sonnet. When it finished the audience applauded and John Rhys-Davies (Gimli) took a deep bow.

The Waiau River, which flows from Lake Te Anau to Lake Manapouri was used to portray the majestic River Anduin in *The Fellowship of the Ring*. Its bush-clad banks were used for the first part of the Fellowship's long river journey to the Brown Lands, the desolate and treeless area between Mirkwood and the Emyn Muil, where long ago the Ent Wives made their gardens. Sections of the river are accessible from the main Te Anau–Manapouri Road.

A more physically challenging option for people who like that sort of thing and have three to four days is the 67 km Kepler Track, commencing in Te Anau. The tramp follows lake edges, through beech forests, over mountaintops and through a U-shaped glacial valley. If that doesn't sound like you, take the main Te Anau–Manapouri highway and turn right at the DOC Rainbow Reach sign onto an unsealed road. As the road veers left (and before it veers right again), turn right down the unmarked track for a superb view of the River Anduin. A further 2 km down the road, a swing bridge crosses the river and you can take a much shorter walk on the Kepler Track. The journey is 10.9 km one way, but even a short stroll will take you into the native beech forest and provide beautiful views of the river. More information on the Kepler Track can be obtained from the local DOC Headquarters in Te Anau.

Mist swirls around the peaks surrounding Lake Manapouri.

Invercargill

Internet:
www.southlandnz.com

Graves in the Eastern Cemetery.

Invercargill is New Zealand's southernmost city. Of Scottish origin, this prosperous city serves a wide agricultural area, with abundant pasture which benefits from the evenly spread annual rainfall.

The sea off the southern coast is home to a prized New Zealand delicacy — the Bluff oyster. Every year visitors from around New Zealand pay homage to this exquisite shellfish at the Bluff Oyster and Southland Seafood Festival.

A walk around the city centre reveals a wealth of Victorian, Edwardian and Art Deco architectural styles. One of these, the Civic Theatre (built in 1906 in the English Renaissance style), hosted the world première of *The World's Fastest Indian*.

The 80 ha Queens Park is a delight, particularly in spring when multicoloured tulips reach up to trees heavy with blossom.

This city also marks the end of John and the Mini's epic journey in *Goodbye Pork Pie*. Leaving Invercargill on SH1, you'll pass the Eastern Cemetery on your right approximately 3 km from the city centre. Here the police roadblock was set up to stop them, but instead the police could only watch as the Mini escaped through the narrow lanes between the gravestones.

Day one of shooting provided a hint of the impact the Invercargill summer weather was to have for five of our six-week shoot — 9 degree temperatures and horizontal rain with bursts of sunshine that would test our endurance, patience and most of all the schedule.

Angered but undaunted by the weather, Roger soon demonstrated (and reminded me of) his powerful, focussed approach to directing: 'No Mike, I don't like a radio headphone, I need a good pair of headphones fed straight from your mixer!'

Mike Westgate, Sound Recordist, *The World's Fastest Indian* (On Film)

I mean, I wanted to make this movie because it was about New Zealand, and I didn't think I'd ever find a more New Zealand story than that of Burt Munro coming to America which had some relevance for me as well, you know…

My experience of coming to America as a stranger — there were a lot of similarities I was able to explore in this movie about my own feelings about New Zealand and America, and getting out into the big wide world and realising how big it really was. And at the same time, about that sort of optimism you have coming from a country like New Zealand.

Roger Donaldson, Producer, *The World's Fastest Indian* (On Film)

Invercargill mayor Tim Shadbolt gathered every councillor into a meeting with myself, production manager Nikki Baigent and location manager Jock Fyfe, and said: 'We are all here and we want this to work for you, the filmmakers, and us, the council, so how can we help?'

We then went through the shooting schedule and explained every step of the way and everybody knew exactly what was required for every shoot day.

Road closures were commonplace and disruption to the city was at times quite heavy but because of that initial meeting everybody knew what was going on … It's called communication.

Murray Francis, Line Producer, *The World's Fastest Indian* (On Film)

Tulips announce the arrival of spring in Queens Park.

The Civic Theatre basks in the sun proudly promoting her world première of *The World's Fastest Indian*.

Oreti Beach

A 15-minute drive from Invercargill will take you to historic Oreti Beach. Stretching over 26 km from Riverton in the north to the New River Estuary in the south, this flat sand beach has witnessed at least two examples of Kiwi ingenuity.

In 1902 Herbert John Pither arrived in Invercargill from Christchurch in a car he had built himself. Setting up an engineering business, he began work on his own aeroplane design. On 5 July 1910, this design apparently took to the air from Oreti Beach to claim the first aerial ascent in New Zealand. Unfortunately there were no witnesses, so this early attempt at aviation remains as a 'possible' only. Recently a replica of the original aircraft has been built and flown successfully — proving his design was capable of flight, and adding considerable credibility to his claim.

As Pither was getting airborne, a young Southlander named Burt Munro was developing an interest in motorcycles. By 1920 he has saved enough money to buy his first Indian motorbike — some 47 years later this man achieved a class speed record of 183.586 mph on the Bonneville Salt Flats in Utah. Burt Munro now owned *The World's Fastest Indian*.

Oreti Beach was used as the proving ground for all of Munro's modifications to his Indian. In 2004 Sir Anthony Hopkins donned helmet and gloves and recreated these runs as filming commenced for *The World's Fastest Indian*.

Tyre marks on Oreti Beach indicate more than just Burt have raced on the hard sands.

Riverton and Winton

A diversion to the picturesque seaside village of Riverton, 40 km from Invercargill on SH99, is a great way to spend an afternoon. The oldest community in Southland, Riverton was inhabited by whalers in the early 1800s. The town still has a nautical feel as fishing boats moor in the tidal estuary and children swim nearby. Visit the area known locally as The Rocks; this gentle bay has a safe swimming beach, rock pools to explore, and a wonderful seafood café.

Riverton is a very popular spot for locals and visitors alike. The safe sandy beaches and rock pools combine to create a relaxing afternoon.

The rolling green hills of Southland provide a rich harvest for newborn lambs in springtime.

The town of Winton, 32 km north of Invercargill, was used in *The World's Fastest Indian* to portray Burt Munro visiting his local bank to borrow money.

Catlins Coast

Internet:
www.catlins.org.nz

The coastal road from Invercargill to Balclutha through the Catlins is part of the Southern Scenic Route and is a journey best undertaken over a couple of days, although the drive can be achieved in four hours.

The area is stunning, featuring dramatic sea cliffs, abundant wildlife and extensive native rainforest. At Curio Bay a forest that flourished 150 million years ago still exists in petrified form, and all along the route there are opportunities to see the rare Hector's dolphin, yellow-eyed penguin and New Zealand sea lions in their natural habitat.

The great castle of Cair Paravel on the Eastern Sea of Narnia in **_The Chronicles of Narnia: The Lion, The Witch and The Wardrobe_** was created on the cliff tops of Purakaunui Bay in the Catlins by computer-generated imagery. Situated 20 km southeast of Owaka, the beach is a favourite with surfers. During a southerly squall this dramatic coast appears to be from a mythical past, as rain lashes the cliffs between spells of bright sunshine that illuminate the cliffs' magical white faces.

For the film, a helicopter with front-mounted space-cam captured the imagery to allow the castle and swimming sea creatures to be added by the computer specialists in Hollywood.

Another use for a microwave. No more defrosting for this one as it collects mail outside a crib (holiday home).

The rolling surf at Purakaunui Bay is a favourite with surfers.

Known as The Edinburgh of the South, Dunedin has many reminders of its Scottish forebears — its name is ancient Gaelic for Edinburgh. The migration of Scots settlers in the 1800s left a legacy of fine Victorian architecture and educational brilliance, a reflection of Dunedin's heyday as the commercial hub of the country, which lasted until the late 1800s. The city housed the first university in New Zealand, and its daily newspaper (the *Otago Daily Times*, founded in 1861) has the longest record of continuous daily publication in the country.

Today, a Scottish shop still sells souvenirs of the city's northern relatives, and students (known locally as Scarfies) provide a diverse mix of study and rebellion, and support a thriving café and restaurant culture.

The city's architecture remains one of its major attractions and a must-see list should include the First Church, the finest railway station in the country, Olveston Stately Home, St Paul's Anglican Cathedral, the college buildings of Otago Boys High School, and the university.

It is against this backdrop that the film *Scarfies* is set. A number of downtown locations were used; as well as the students' home, set amongst a wonderful collection of Tudor-, Jacobean- and Georgian-styled dwellings. The actual flat used in filming is situated on Brown Street, looking down towards The Octagon.

Dunedin

Internet:
www.dunedinnz.com

The Dunedin Railway Station was opened in 1906 and at the time was the busiest in the country. Of very ornate design, its architect George A. Troup was the first architect of New Zealand Railways. Its Flemish Renaissance style accorded the following quotation in the *Evening Star* newspaper of the time: *The ornamentation of the ceilings is delicate, and the whole atmosphere of the place is one of costliness … the lavatory and sanitary arrangements are luxurious.*

Otago Harbour is well worth exploration, with rolling hills enclosed by stone walls revealing glimpses of the harbour which are certainly reminiscent of Scotland, and one of the areas Peter Jackson considered for Hobbiton. A peninsula tour provides an interesting potpourri of attractions. Glenfalloch (Gaelic for Hidden Valley) has a wonderful collection of rhododendrons, azaleas and magnolias that blend well with stands of mature oak, walnut, elm and New Zealand natives. At Portobello there is a fine restaurant, and a little further down the road is Taiaroa Head. The Heads have an interesting military history and are home to the only mainland colony of albatross in the world. Nearby Larnach Castle is worth a visit on your return, with sweeping views of Dunedin city from high on the hills.

The calm waters of Otago Harbour hardly ever ruffle and are popular for yachting, kayaking and windsurfing.

Above: If the Mini had slowed down in *Goodbye Pork Pie*, this is the view the boys would have had as they crossed Mt Cargill to descend towards Port Chalmers.

Left: This small cottage at Deborah Bay has seen many children pass through her doors. Within this cottage and small shed lived 17 children at one time — the 11 boys slept in the shed whilst the girls slept inside.

If you are driving north from Dunedin, a good scenic route is via Port Chalmers, departing Dunedin on SH88. The Port itself saw the arrival of Dunedin's first settlers in 1848 and the departure of the first frozen-meat shipment to Britain in 1882. Clinging to the hills is St Iona's Presbyterian Church. Built in 1883, its dour face would have looked across to see the departure of Antarctic explorers Scott, Shackleton and Byrd as they headed south to the ice.

Taking the road marked Waitati, there are spectacular views of the harbour as you climb over Mt Cargill and down to the intersection with SH1 again. As you join SH1, and with a careful eye on the traffic, spare a glance for the intersection itself. It was here that a very eccentric and slightly drug-crazed Snout led our heroes towards false safety in *Goodbye Pork Pie*.

The Tuapeka Ferry.

Central Otago

Internet:
www.centralotagonz.com

For me, filmmaking is not only about telling stories but to convey a palpable sense of another person's world — how they experience things, not just what they do. I knew at the outset of making *In My Father's Den* that I wanted to make an intimate and subjective film about a damaged soul, that began gently — almost too quietly — which slowly (almost invisibly) became an edgy and unrelenting mystery, culminating in a violent confrontation between the past and the present. I intended the film to be a 'slow burner' and avoided setting it up as a 'thriller' or 'missing person story', opting more for a personal and character-driven approach. I wanted to create a subtle sense of disquiet and a strong sense of place, to play with shifting time-frames. I also wanted to create a sense of interconnecting lives and the past and present being strongly intertwined ...

I see small towns as being dangerously intimate. I think character is born of place as much as it is of anything else. People and place are something I'm interested in exploring ... We'll quite often mythologise landscape — people think of us as being in this exotic landscape — but to me it's full of texture and there's a beauty, but there's also a darkness, and I think the expansiveness is tempered by a sort of claustrophobic element.

Brad McGann, Director, *In My Father's Den*

"We carefully scheduled the film at a time when it would benefit from the fact that different types of fruit trees come into blossom at different times, such that winter, spring and even summer sequences could be shot within the same time period and in the same general area."
Trevor Haysom, Producer, *In My Father's Den*

Central Otago is a region of stark contrasts both within its landscapes and seasons. Green pastures give way to orchards and vineyards which grow superb Pinot Noir grapes amidst rocky outcrops of schist rock. In winter the days are a magical combination of crunchy frost and blue skies, whilst in summer the area swelters under an intense dry heat.

It is appropriate that one of the opening scenes of *In My Father's Den* features a train. The railway was an integral part of the landscape for over 70 years, and remains one of the most breathtaking ways to see the region. Although regular services ceased in 1990, some track remains as the Taieri Gorge tourist railway. The company operates a daily service from Dunedin to Middlemarch through the tortuous Taieri River Gorge across wrought-iron viaducts and through tunnels carved by hand more than 100 years ago. This train and track are shown when Paul travels to his father's funeral and Celia lies on the track as the train roars past on the adjacent line.

The town that features in this film is Roxburgh, named after an ancient ruined town on the banks of the Teviot River in Scotland. Sitting quietly on the banks of the Clutha River, Roxburgh is the centre of a large fruit-growing region. The house Paul lives in is normally inhabited by seasonal fruit-pickers

Above: Instead of railway carriages, sheep now graze in the shade of the Teviot goods shed close to Roxburgh.

Right: The Presbyterian Church, Roxburgh.

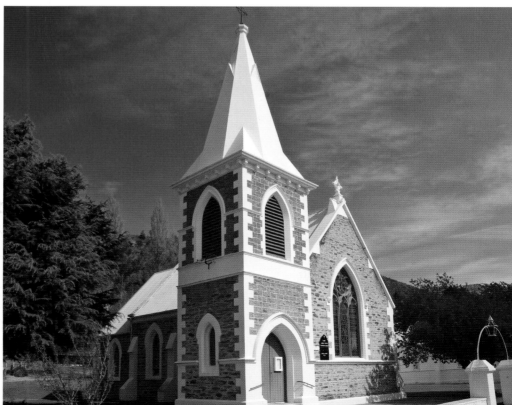

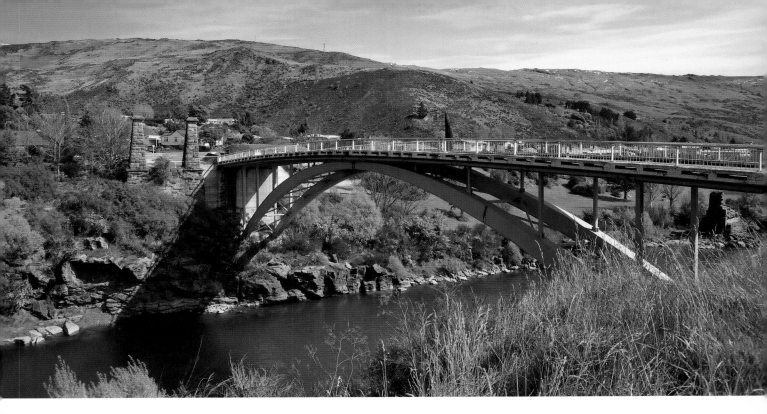

and most of the orchard scenes were filmed between Ettrick and Roxburgh. Opposite the area school in town is the Presbyterian Church (scene of the funeral), built in 1880.

Driving down to the Clutha River bank, an elegant single-span bridge crossing the river can be seen, which Celia crossed on her motor scooter.

Heading further inland on SH8 the road leaves Roxburgh through a sea of orchards, where the parade of seasons is so vivid in a country where native trees are evergreen. Spring carpets the trees in blossom, that flow into the warm colours of sun-ripened apricots and peaches in summer, before autumn arrives with her swirling fog and rich colours of russet and gold. The icy tendrils of a brittle hoar frost and the white blanket of winter snow finish the seasonal succession.

As you pass the Roxburgh Hydro Station on your right, rugged Central Otago schist takes over as the road climbs for majestic views of the Clutha flowing hundreds of metres below.

At Fruitlands, a carefully restored stone cottage is the perfect place for a coffee before Butcher's Dam, where Celia sat and reflected on the side of the dam. The town of Alexandra is a further five minutes away.

The Clutha River at Roxburgh. The second longest river in New Zealand, the Clutha is one of the swiftest for its size in the world, with a number of man-made lakes supplying electricity to the national grid.

Snow can fall at any time in the mountains of Central Otago. The heat of the valley distorts an early snowfall on the St Bathan's Range.

Blossoms announce the arrival of spring in Roxburgh.

The lure of gold in 1862 brought European settlers to the region, but as the easily won gold was soon depleted the population decreased, until the 1890s when the idea of dredging for gold saw a resurgence in population of nearby Alexandra. When the dredging began to dwindle, residents discovered the soil was rich in potash and phosphoric acid and fruit orchards became the new gold.

Alexandra is the main service town for the Central Otago Region and has a number of attractions related to the gold fields. Very popular in summer, it has the distinction of the lowest rainfall of any town in New Zealand.

The township of Clyde still has a number of original buildings from the 1800s, serving wonderful food incorporating the best in local produce, and in 1999 a street party celebrated the end of filming of **The Two Towers** at nearby Poolburn.

A great way to explore this region is via the Central Otago Rail Trail. Although the trains have now gone, 150 km of track from Clyde to Middlemarch has been converted into a trail for bikes, horses or pedestrians. While easily accessible from the road for a day trip, to really savour the spectacular scenery, consider hiring a cycle and stopping overnight at one of the small country hotels en route.

The rail trail (or road for the less energetic) from Clyde on SH85 takes you north through rugged rock country towards the country town of Omakau. This unlikely location housed production offices for both *The Two Towers* and *Fifty Ways of Saying Fabulous*.

Just before Omakau, a gravel road will take you to the village of Ophir, the main location for *Fifty Ways of Saying Fabulous*. A one-way suspension bridge is the perfect entrance to this town that has let time pass it by. Holding the New Zealand record for the coldest and hottest temperatures, Ophir has some of the best preserved buildings from our past; ready-made sets for the 1970s setting of *Fifty Ways of Saying Fabulous*.

> We had a production office in Omakau, hut editing was set up in Ophir, a five-minute drive away. I shared the Ophir Peace Memorial Hall with Kirsty Cameron's wardrobe department. When I arrived in Ophir, line producer Dorthe Scheffman suggested that the front room in the hall, which faced north, might be too hot (the crew were stripping off to cool down in the river), so I set up on the stage of the hall, with wardrobe on the floor beneath me. It snowed in the hills the next day, so it got pretty cold sometimes.
>
> Peter Roberts, Editor, *Fifty Ways of Saying Fabulous*

Above: The Ophir Memorial Hall reflects on the social effects of war.

Below: Butcher's Dam near Fruitlands. The dam itself is accessible via a short walk from the car park. Celia sat and dangled her feet over the edge here in *In My Father's Den*.

To reach Rohan as filmed for *The Two Towers*, take the road from Ophir towards Poolburn. As the road climbs over The Raggedy Range, pause at the top for dramatic views of a land seemingly untouched by human hand. It was here that scenes from *In My Father's Den* of Paul and Celia sitting amongst the rocks with Paul's Triumph 2500 parked below were filmed.

Left: The Daniel O'Connell suspension bridge has carried travellers across the Manuherikia River since 1880. Spanning 65.6 m, the suspended span saw the Triumph cross over in *In My Father's Den*.

Above: The existing small cribs (holiday homes) around the lake were cleverly disguised as outbuildings in *The Two Towers*.

Right: Wooden posts are all that remain of the Rohirrim village viciously attacked by Orcs and wildmen in *The Two Towers*.

Below: One of the most remote and scenic toilets in New Zealand, perched on the side of the lake.

The sky is usually an intense blue, and in summer the shimmering heat haze distorts distance into a golden sphere. After descending to the valley floor, turn right at the Poolburn Hotel onto Moa Creek Road and continue on to Webster Lane, where you need to turn left into the unpaved road. The climb to Poolburn itself commences beside Bonspiel Station.

Poolburn Dam was completed in 1931, as a storage lake to irrigate the Ida Valley below. The land is rich and during the height of the gold rush there were five hotels dispensing liquid warmth to miners toiling in the harsh environment. Today it's a popular recreational area and the reservoir is richly stocked with brown trout.

On reaching the lake, there is an excellent view across to the location of the small village in *The Two Towers* where Morwen sent her children to safety on horseback. Small traces of the village remain and the area is immediately recognisable.

A number of other sites were used in this locality to show Merry and Pippin being rushed to Saruman and the epic chase by Aragorn, Gimli and Legolas.

When I teamed up with writer/director Glenn Standring we were both living in Dunedin and sick of travelling away from home and families for work. Glenn had written *Perfect Creature* some time ago and I was immediately taken with its originality and the requirement for a unique look and feel. We describe it as a science fiction thriller set in an alternate retro-futuristic world.

We knew Dunedin had fantastic Victorian architecture which was well preserved and, in most cases, still fully functioning. Just living in the city meant we knew lots of probable locations for the film once we were greenlit. We would meet for coffee in the Octagon then walk around the key city centre blocks and identify this street or that building as being contenders for certain scenes.

Once we locked our finance around early 2004, we conducted specific scouts with Heads of Department such as Director of Photography Leon Narbey, Production Designer Phil Ivey and Assistant Director Liz Tan. We had well-known South Island Location Manager Harry Whitehurst working with us, so we started looking around corners and down alleyways and suddenly a whole new city opened up. Behind the façades and busy city streets there exists a hidden world of original, intact brick and stone alleys, streets, building façades and cul-de-sacs. It was like stepping into mini Dickensian London backstreets.

At Harry's suggestion, we travelled to Oamaru to check out the historic precinct. We were a little reluctant at first because it was about an hour's drive from Dunedin and we didn't want to lose valuable shooting time on the road.

When we got there though, we realised we had to come up with a schedule which took us to Oamaru because it offered fantastic 360-degree period exterior buildings and streets, crossroads and had a truly authentic feel. So we got the 'retro' in Dunedin and Oamaru and our Art Department gave us the 'futuristic' in conjunction with our digital FX team.

Nearly as important as the look is the strong support and assistance of the people and the authorities in both towns. The respective City Councils were truly behind us and the people were brilliant as extras, as suppliers or as friends.

The shoot went incredibly smoothly, cast, crew and locals had a great time and Glenn and I look forward to shooting at least part of our next film in our home town area.

Tim Sanders, Producer, *Perfect Creature*

Oamaru

Internet:
www.tourismwaitaki.co.nz

Swords and heraldry for the great lion Aslan.

The ancient Elephant Rocks that burst from the rolling hills in the Waitaki district of the South Island were transformed in 2004 into Aslan's Camp in *The Lion, The Witch and The Wardrobe*, first of the *Chronicles of Narnia* to be filmed.

The historic town of Oamaru is the ideal base for exploring the area. Here Victorian buildings crafted from the local white limestone still stand as a reminder of times gone by. Originally built as warehouses and storage areas for the nearby port, the Harbour/Tyne area is now home to antique shops, gift stores, restaurants and craftsmen.

The hidden valley at Elephant Rocks was transformed into a celebration of silk as Aslan gathered his army in *The Lion, The Witch and The Wardrobe*.

A 'dummy' Aslan is used as a placeholder prior to computer generation during filming at Elephant Rocks.

Close by is the Oamaru blue penguin colony. The smallest of their kind in the world, the blue penguins nest beside Oamaru Harbour and can be viewed in their natural habitat.

Oamaru is also home to the award-winning Whitestone Cheese, and the factory has an onsite café and shop allowing visitors to sample local wine and produce.

Elephant Rocks are a 40-minute drive from Oamaru on SH83, near Duntroon. Over 24 million years ago this whole area was under the sea. Whales and other marine life sank into the soft sand which then rose to the surface during the past few million years. The result is an intriguing area of fossils and dramatic limestone outcrops, very effectively covered by The Vanished World visitor centre in Duntroon, which houses interpretive displays on the area's geological past, and is highly reccommended. Trail maps are available with directions to Elephant Rocks.

Named after Twizel Bridge in Northumberland, the town was built to house the thousands of workers who descended on the area in the 1970s to construct the Upper Waitaki Power Scheme. The majority of workers have since gone, but the town is now a popular holiday destination with the nearby Lake Ohau and its associated ski-field. Close by is the man-made Lake Ruataniwha which yields both rainbow and brown trout.

Snuggled under the foothills of the Southern Alps, the region is one of extreme weather conditions as snow cloaks the area in winter while hot summer winds can bring temperatures of over 30°C.

There is a wide variety of accommodation and restaurants available in town, as well as a well-equipped camping ground and numerous farm home-stays.

The largest battle scene filmed in *The Lord of the Rings Trilogy* was the Battle of the Pelennor Fields, filmed near Twizel. It provided a perfect combination — snow-covered mountain peaks, grassy fields, a remote location (with no pre-existing signs of habitation) and a town close enough to provide necessary infrastructure.

Organised tours are the only way to visit the locations, which are all on private land. These can be booked from the local Visitor Information Centre and come highly recommended — your tour guide will most likely have taken part in the filming. As well as viewing the magnificent scenery, you'll hear a first-hand account of filming more than 200 horses in majestic battle scenes. As an added bonus, you'll also receive an insight into the demanding life of high-country farmers living in a stunning but very harsh and unforgiving environment.

Twizel

Internet:
www.mtcook.org.nz

Gandalf and Pippin were filmed crossing a small stream here near Twizel.

Aoraki (Mt Cook)

Internet:
www.mtcook.org.nz

Aoraki (Mt Cook) seen from The Hermitage.

Mt Potts

Internet:
www.christchurchnz.net

Mt Sunday appears in the centre distance.

After visiting Twizel, drive up to the alpine village of The Hermitage, just 106 km from Tekapo and nestled under the Southern Alps in Mt Cook National Park, where Aoraki (Mt Cook) is surrounded by the highest peaks in New Zealand. First climbed on Christmas Day 1894 by three Christchurch men, its challenging ridges provided a training ground for world-famous New Zealand mountaineer, Sir Edmund Hillary, prior to his ascent of Mt Everest.

From The Hermitage there are a number of alpine walks with wonderful views. A highlight is a scenic ski-plane flight from the local airport taking you over the mountains for a snow landing high up on the Tasman Glacier.

If time is limited, one of the best walks is through the Hooker Flats. Allow four hours return to amble through bush on a well-formed track to Sefton Stream with a view of the terminal moraine of the Hooker Glacier.

The Hermitage is a real treat — with magnificent lodgings dwarfed by the 'Misty Mountains'. Nearby Glentanner Park also has accommodation, or alternatively you can return to Twizel.

Over millennia, the snow-fed Rangitata River has formed an alluvial shingle fan, virtually surrounded by the Southern Alps. Ancient glaciers deposited rocky outcrops amidst the shingle and Mt Sunday, the location for the Rohirrim stronghold of Edoras and Meduseld, King Theoden's hall, in Tolkien's realm of Rohan, was one of these. The evocation of Tolkien's land of the Horse Lords and the Riders of Rohan became one of the most memorable images in ***The Two Towers***.

As the road descends into the Rangitata Valley, Mt Sunday is ahead of you, in isolated splendour amidst brown tussock and the intertwined tributaries of the braided river. With no access to the mountain, the best views are from the unpaved road at the entrance to Mt Potts Station.

Edoras took eleven months to complete and caused quite a stir as fans armed with cameras and binoculars tried to catch a glimpse of the emerging set. One enterprising journalist hired a light aircraft to complete a photographic scoop, with his images published worldwide.

A working high-country station of 2700 ha, Mt Potts stretches from an altitude of 500 m to 2300 m and is home to flocks of hardy New Zealand merino sheep. Accommodation in an alpine lodge or cottages on the station provides an experience of life in the high-country, with delicious home-cooked meals. In winter, skiing and snowboarding are popular, along with tramping, fishing or simply relaxing in stunningly beautiful surroundings.

Arthur's Pass

High in the Southern Alps of the South Island is an area of tortured rocks and dramatic valleys known as Flock Hill, where director Andrew Adamson filmed the great battle for Narnia in *The Lion, The Witch and The Wardrobe*. The actual area where filming was undertaken is on private land, but tours are available with Canterbury Sightseeing.

Flock Hill is situated 90 minutes from Christchurch on the Arthur's Pass Highway to Greymouth. Leaving Christchurch, the South Island's largest city, the road crosses the flat expanse of the Canterbury Plains through the small towns of Darfield and Sheffield. At Springfield the mountain peaks tower over the village and the road climbs dramatically to Porter's Pass (942 m). One of the highest passes in New Zealand, the road can be affected by snow in winter. Lake Lyndon, surrounded by brown tussock hills, is well worth a stop before continuing past Castle Hill to Flock Hill.

Stop at Cave Stream Scenic Reserve by Broken River, where limestone rocks seen from here and across Cave Stream are typical of the landscape used to portray Narnia.

It has this fantastic landscape, and it is perfect for Narnia. It was quite extraordinarily apt for us — I suspect people may assume some of the landscapes are actually computer-generated images, but that isn't the case. It looks a bit like a mythical Scotland, actually, and it is quite an extraordinary place. Andrew is a Kiwi himself, and for sure it must have made financial sense, but it was a wonderful place to go and work.

Tilda Swinton, The White Witch

There are two walking tracks from the car park. One leads to the upstream entrance to Cave Stream before entering the 362 m water-filled tunnel, while the other leads to a view of the outfall.

Accommodation is available at Flock Hill Station, a further 10-minute drive. Other activities available in the area include abseiling, rock climbing, tramping and canyoning. In winter, skiing and snowboarding abounds at the nearby Broken River, Craigieburn, Mt Cheeseman, Porter Heights and Temple Basin ski-fields.

For those travelling to the West Coast, the Tranz Alpine train is an excellent way to view this mountainous scenery. Run as a daily service from Christchurch to Greymouth, the trip is one of the best railway journeys in the world. This was the track used in *Goodbye Pork Pie* as our travellers crossed the main divide.

www.
lionwitchwardrobetours.co.nz

Previous: Filming of Narnia in such a remote place required a huge support team. A tent city to feed over 500 people sprang up out of 'camera' and stayed during the six weeks of filming of **The Lion, The Witch and The Wardrobe**.

Opposite: 'Chariot Run' at Flock Hill. Normally the abode of New Zealand native falcon, satyrs, cyclops and centaur reigned for a brief period in 2004.

Below: The stunning green paddock at Flock Hill that was used in the final battle scene of **The Lion, The Witch and The Wardrobe**. Special grass was planted a year before filming and watered carefully to create a green oases instead of the normal brown tussocks.

Overleaf: During filming in early December 2004 an amazing late snowfall created a suggestion that the supremacy of The White Witch was not over.

The 'Garden City' of Christchurch certainly lives up to its name. No matter where you walk or drive, there always seems to be a park or expansive garden nearby. The city also demonstrates strong visual links with its English heritage, with buildings that could have been transplanted directly from London or Oxford. During 1850–51 organised groups of English settlers arrived on the First Four Ships in Lyttelton Harbour, and it is from these pioneering beginnings that this city of 340,000 people was born.

Plan to spend a few days in Christchurch to visit the excellent museum and art gallery, taste the great food on offer and walk the wide streets and gardens.

A good place to start a walking tour of the city is Cathedral Square, the centre of the city with the imposing Christchurch cathedral taking centre stage. Immigrants who arrived from England in the 1800s from England modelled their fledgling city on Christ Church, Oxford, and in 1858, the first Bishop of Christchurch (Henry Harper) attended a meeting where plans and the building of a cathedral were agreed. The first foundation stone was laid in 1864, and by 1881 the nave was opened to great public fanfare. After another 23 years the cathedral was finally completed in 1904, to become the most visited church in New Zealand.

Christchurch

www.christchurchnz.net

Above: A giant game of chess is played out under the watchful eye of Christchurch Cathedral.

Left: The Citizens War Memorial in Cathedral Square was unveiled in 1937. The six figures represent youth, justice, peace, sacrifice, valour and victory.

Far left: Statue of Jesus with the Christchurch Cathedral behind.

Make time to climb the stairs to the top of the cathedral tower, for a great view over the Square and city below. The Square is the city's traditional meeting place and until recent years the haunt of the Wizard of Christchurch, an eccentric and much-loved chap who used to speak eloquently on many subjects and humorously berate passersby. He appears in *Goodbye Pork Pie* as Gerry and John return to the railway station and their train trip to the West Coast.

The Arts Centre of Christchurch is another interesting spot to visit, situated a short walk off the square directly down Worcester Street. Originally the University of Canterbury, these buildings are now a vibrant collections of cafés, shops and an excellent weekend market. Shirl danced famously around these cloisters in *Goodbye Pork Pie*.

Every weekend the Christchurch Arts Centre becomes a vibrant market, but there are still plenty of places to find solitude amongst the cloisters. It was within these buildings that New Zealand scientist Ernest Rutherford, famous for splitting the atom, obtained his MA in 1889 before continuing his studies overseas, receiving the 1908 Nobel Prize in Chemistry for his work with radiation and the atomic nucleus.

A 750 m walk up Montreal Street to Cranmer Square will take you to the old Christchurch Girls High School building, situated on the southwest corner of Montreal and Armagh Streets. Christchurch Girls was established in 1878 and ran from the Arts Centre until shifting to these premises in 1882. It is now in new buildings beside the Avon River on the other side of Hagley Park. The opening crane shot of the school in *Heavenly Creatures* was taken from Cranmer Square.

A pleasant return route to the city is via Hagley Park and the museum — both sites appearing in *Heavenly Creatures*.

An excellent way to visit the Arts Centre is by tram, the same as those used in *Heavenly Creatures*.

Victoria Park

Situated about 7 km from the city centre near the top of the Cashmere Hills is Victoria Park. Set aside as a reserve in 1870, extensive planning and planting saw the park formally opened in 1897 to commemorate the Diamond Jubilee of Queen Victoria. You can reach the park by car or bus, just as Pauline and Juliet did in *Heavenly Creatures*.

The tea rooms that appear in the film were torn down soon after filming was completed. Now there is a visitor's centre a little further up the hill with displays of the flora and fauna in the area as well as outlining the many walks.

The steps the girls take Honora Parker down are next to the main car park, where there is a small gate in the hedge, which did not appear in the film. At the bottom of these steps a number of walks branch off in different directions. A very pleasant few hours can be sent walking the leafy paths with views of the city and Pegasus Bay stretching away in the distance. In winter the snow-clad Kaikoura Ranges many kilometres to the north stand like icy sentinels on the horizon.

The stairs Honora went down, never to return, in *Heavenly Creatures*.

Well, *The Frighteners* came about through slightly odd circumstances. We heard that Robert Zemeckis was looking for a film he would direct based on his *Tales from the Crypt* TV series. And we had this idea for a ghost story about a sort of a psychic conman who makes people believe he can see ghosts — he actually can see ghosts but he uses the ghosts to scare people so he gets employed to help rid the people of ghosts ... So, we pitched the idea of our ghost story to him. And he liked it and he said, 'Sure, let's write the script.' So we wrote the script ... then when we delivered the screenplay to him, he said, 'Oh, forget the *Tales from the Crypt* thing' ... He was going off in a different direction with that ... And then he said, 'Well, you know, do you want to make it?' The thing with *The Frighteners* that ended up being the biggest disappointment for us, is that it was originally conceived as a Halloween movie, to be released Halloween week, which is traditional in the States when the sort of ghost movies come out. And then the Stallone movie *Daylight* was delayed for six months and so they decided to bring *The Frighteners* up from Halloween and plonk it into the middle of summer ... it never was and should never have been a summer movie ... I've realised in hindsight that the thinking behind *The Frighteners* was very similar to that behind *Heavenly Creatures*, where you basically use burnout and funny situations to meet the characters you're going to be following. So you get to like them, you get to laugh along with them, and you relax and think, 'These are quite funny people.' And then the screws start to tighten. In the case of *Creatures*, it was when the girls start plotting the murder, and in *The Frighteners* it's when the Grim Reaper figure comes to town and starts to kill people, and Frank has to stop goofing around and get serious about saving lives. The ghosts in *The Frighteners* were played by actors, so we had to shoot them during the live-action filming, but they couldn't be shot at the same time as Michael's scenes because they were transparent and glowing. That meant we had to shoot Michael first, by himself, and then the ghost actors afterwards, against blue screens.

Director Peter Jackson

The Sign of the Takahe was the major building planned by Harry (H. G.) Ell in a series of staging points reaching all the way to Akaroa. He never achieved his dream, and this building stands as a monument to his endeavour.

The Sign of the Takahe

Just down from Victoria Park at 200 Hackthorne Road is the imposing Sign of the Takahe. It was here in *The Frighteners* that Bannister and Dr Lynskey arrived in the pouring rain to have a quiet dinner with a ghost but which ended in another violent death. Opened in 1949, this wonderful old building, which commemorates a number of English building styles, is well worth a visit. A Devonshire tea amongst the heraldry and armour seated in the same room as Bannister is just like being in a live film set.

Internet:
www.bankspeninsula.info

Lyttelton

The Port of Lyttelton overlooks a magnificent harbour, enclosed on two sides by the brown tussock of the Port Hills. Originally called Port Cooper, Te-Whaka-raupo (the harbour of the bulrush reeds) was home to the Maori for over 1000 years. The formation of the Canterbury Association in 1848 and its vision to create a Church of England colony in New Zealand was the catalyst that created the port. A wharf was constructed in 1849 to allow the berthing of the first four ships from England, and since then the port has grown to be the largest in the South Island.

Lyttelton retains a strong sense of its historic past and the weatherboard cottages and stone buildings that cling to the hillside make a real-life visit into an earlier time. It was a ready-made set for Peter Jackson to use as the fictional American town of Fairwater in *The Frighteners*. The Anglican Cemetery was

Left: Shades of Peter Jackson humour. A bar sign in Lyttelton.

Below: Colourful façades welcome diners in the main street of Lyttelton.

used extensively in *The Frighteners*. Situated at the top of Canterbury Street, it is a very steep drive to the location and there is very limited parking. The main gates are on a small feeder drive (with no exit).

A walk through the cemetery reveals the tough life that faced early European immigrants to New Zealand. The inscriptions describing death at an early age are many, and are testimony to the perils of the sea, illness and accidents that plagued those early settlers.

The main street of Lyttelton is a vibrant cosmopolitan mix of locals and sea-faring types of many nationalities. There are a number of excellent cafés and the street looks very similar to 1996, when filming was undertaken. The corner of Canterbury and London Streets is where Bannister bumps into a pierced biker aka Peter Jackson.

Above: The cemetery that appeared in *The Frighteners* holds many memories of those who lost their lives in early pioneering days.

Left: The wharf at Port Levy that provided a delightful springboard to cool waters in *Heavenly Creatures*.

If travelling on to Akaroa, make a stop at the Hilltop Café for great food and views across to Barry's Bay, Duvauchelles and Akaroa itself.

The view from the top of the hill before descending into Okains Bay, and the reverse view back up to the brown tussock hills that almost enclose the harbour.

Banks Peninsula

Banks Peninsula is a diverse landscape of ordered fields, brown tussock hills of considerable height and tranquil bays that have spilled over the breached walls of extinct ancient volcanoes.

One of these remote gorgeous bays is Port Levy, used to shoot the scene where the Hulmes and Pauline spend their Easter holiday in *Heavenly Creatures*.

The best way to reach the location is to drive from Lyttelton around to Diamond Harbour. Many small bays on this drive would make an ideal picnic spot, and close to Diamond Harbour is Orton Bradley Park — a working farm park with tennis courts, golf club, adventure playground, picnic sites and gardens. It is a very popular spot for locals in summer when the norwest wind blows and the mercury rises to over 30°C.

From Diamond Harbour the road climbs steadily to the lip of the extinct volcano with wonderful views of Lyttelton and the harbour. Port Levy on the other side is a small holiday beach settlement, the haunt of whalers and fishermen for many years and also the real site of the Hulme bach.

It plays an important part in the real-life story of Parker and Hulme as well as in the film. The wharf remains as it appears in the film (although repainted) and is a pleasant place to cast a line for fish or watch the clouds roll in from the sea when the wind blows from the east.

There are other roads leaving Port Levy for Akaroa and Pigeon Bay, but they are very steep and narrow and not recommended. Instead return to Diamond Harbour and continue around to the delightful historic French settlement of Akaroa. This trip and the return to Christchurch can be accomplished in one day.

Location New Zealand

Location New Zealand

Location New Zealand

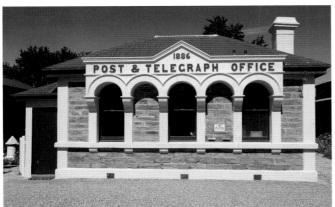

1939
REWI'S LAST STAND Director: Rudall Hayward

1949
THE SANDS OF IWA JIMA (locations)
    Director: Allan Dwan

1952
BROKEN BARRIER Directors: John O'Shea /
    Roger Mirams

1954
THE SEEKERS (locations) Director: Ken Annakin

1957
UNTIL THEY SAIL (locations) Director: Robert Wise

1962
RUNAWAY Director: John O'Shea

1964
DON'T LET IT GET YOU Director: John O'Shea

1969
YOUNG GUY ON MT. COOK (locations)
    Director: Jun Fukuda

1972
TO LOVE A MAORI (16mm) Director: Rudall Hayward

1973
RANGI'S CATCH (locations) Director: Michael Forlong

1974
GAMES '74 Directors: John King, Sam Pillsbury, Paul
    Maunder, Arthur Everard

1975
TEST PICTURES: ELEVEN VIGNETTES FROM A
    RELATIONSHIP (16mm) Director: Geoff Steven
LANDFALL (16mm) Director: Paul Maunder

1976
OFF THE EDGE Director: Michael Firth
THE GOD BOY Director: Murray Reece

1977
WILD MAN Director: Geoff Murphy
SLEEPING DOGS Director: Roger Donaldson
SOLO Director: Tony Williams

1978
DIED IN THE WOOL Director: Brian McDuffie
COLOUR SCHEME Director: Peter Sharp

1979
JACK WINTER'S DREAM Director: David Sims
ANGEL MINE Director: David Blyth

SKINDEEP Director: Geoff Steven
MIDDLE AGE SPREAD (16mm) Director: John Reid
SONS FOR THE RETURN HOME Director: Paul
    Maunder

1980
GOODBYE PORK PIE Director: Geoff Murphy
BEYOND REASONABLE DOUBT
    Director: John Laing
SQUEEZE (16mm) Director: Richard Turner

1981
WILDCAT (16mm) Directors: Ross Prosser, Russell
    Campbell, Alister Barry
RACE FOR THE YANKEE ZEPHYR
    Director: David Hemmings
PICTURES Director: Michael Black
STRANGE BEHAVIOUR/DEAD KIDS/
    SHADOWLAND Director: Michael Laughlin
BAD BLOOD (locations) Director: Mike Newell
SMASH PALACE Director: Roger Donaldson

1982
HANG ON A MINUTE MATE Director: Alan Lindsay
UTU Director: Geoff Murphy
BATTLETRUCK Director: Harley Cokliss
CARRY ME BACK Director: John Reid
BROTHERS (locations) Director: Terry Bourke
PRISONER (locations) Director: Peter Werner
THE SCARECROW Director: Sam Pillsbury

1983
IT'S LIZZIE TO THOSE CLOSE (16mm)
    Director: David Blyth
WAR YEARS Director: Pat McGuire
CONSTANCE Director: Bruce Morrison
WILD HORSES Director: Derek Morton
SAVAGE ISLANDS Director: Ferdinand Fairfax
STRATA Director: Geoff Steven
THE LOST TRIBE Director: John Laing
PATU Director: Merata Mita
SECOND TIME LUCKY (locations)
    Director: Michael Anderson
HEART OF THE STAG Director: Michael Firth
MERRY CHRISTMAS MR LAWRENCE
    (locations) Director: Nagisa Oshima
TRESPASSES Director: Peter Sharp
AMONG THE CINDERS Director: Rolf Haedrich
IRIS Director: Tony Isaac
THE BOUNTY (locations) Director: Roger Donaldson
SHAKER RUN Director: Bruce Morrison
DEATH WARMED UP Director: David Blyth
HOT TARGET (locations) Director: Denis Lewiston
MR WRONG Director: Gaylene Preston
THE QUIET EARTH Director: Geoff Murphy
LIE OF THE LAND Director: Grahame McLean
SHOULD I BE GOOD Director: Grahame McLean
CAME A HOT FRIDAY Director: Ian Mune

OTHER HALVES Director: John Laing
LEAVE ALL FAIR Director: John Reid
PALLET ON THE FLOOR Director: Lynton Butler
TRIAL RUN Director: Melanie Read
SYLVIA Director: Michael Firth
MESMERIZED (locations) Director: Michael Laughlin
KINGPIN Director: Mike Walker
VIGIL Director: Vincent Ward
THE SILENT ONE Director: Yvonne Mackay

1985
QUEEN CITY ROCKER Director: Bruce Morrison
BRIDGE TO NOWHERE Director: Ian Mune
DANGEROUS ORPHANS Director: John Laing

1986
ARRIVING TUESDAY Director: Richard Riddiford
THE NEGLECTED MIRACLE Director: Barry Barclay
NGATI Director: Barry Barclay
ACES GO PLACES IV (locations) Director: Ringo Lam
AGAINST THE LAW (locations) Director: Ringo Lam
FOOTROT FLATS Director: Murray Ball

1987
THE RESCUE (locations) Director: Ferdinand Fairfax
MARK II (16mm) Director: John Anderson
ILLUSTRIOUS ENERGY Director: Leon Narbey
MAURI Director: Merata Mita
THE LEADING EDGE Director: Michael Firth
BAD TASTE Director: Peter Jackson
WILLOW (locations) Director: Ron Howard
STARLIGHT HOTEL Director: Sam Pillsbury
THE NAVIGATOR Director: Vincent Ward

1988
THE CHILL FACTOR Director: David L. Stanton
NEVER SAY DIE Director: Geoff Murphy
THE GRASSCUTTER Director: Ian Mune
A SOLDIER'S TALE Director: Larry Parr
SEND A GORILLA Director: Melanie Read
ZILCH! Director: Richard Riddiford

1989
USER FRIENDLY Director: Gregor Nicholas
CHAMPION Director: Peter Sharp
FLYING FOX IN A FREEDOM TREE
    Director: Martyn Sanderson
SHRIMP ON THE BARBIE Director: Michael Gottlieb
MEET THE FEEBLES Director: Peter Jackson
WILDFIRE Director: Henri Safran

1990
MANA WAKA Director: Merata Mita
TE RUA Director: Barry Barclay
RUBY AND RATA Director: Gaylene Preston
AN ANGEL AT MY TABLE Director: Jane Campion
EXPOSURE Director: David Blyth
NO ONE CAN HEAR YOU Director: John Laing

THE RETURNING Director: John Day
UNDERCOVER Director: Yvonne Mackay

1991
OLD SCORES Director: Alan Clayton
CHUNUK BAIR Director: Dale Bradley
MOONRISE Director: David Blyth
THE END OF THE GOLDEN WEATHER
    Director: Ian Mune
SECRETS Director: Michael Pattinson

1992
CRUSH Director: Alison Maclean
THE PIANO Director: Jane Campion
ABSENT WITHOUT LEAVE Director: John Laing
THE FOOTSTEP MAN Director: Leon Narbey
ALEX Director: Megan Simpson
BRAINDEAD Director: Peter Jackson

1993
TYPHON'S PEOPLE Director: Yvonne Mackay
ADRIFT (US telemovie)
JACK BE NIMBLE Director: Garth Maxwell
BREAD AND ROSES (16mm) Director: Gaylene Preston
COPS AND ROBBERS Director: Murray Reece
DESPERATE REMEDIES Director: Stewart Main/
    Peter Wells

1994
HERCULES (4 x telemovies)
LOADED Director: Anna Campion
THE LAST TATTOO Director: John Reid
ONCE WERE WARRIORS Director: Lee Tamahori
HEAVENLY CREATURES Director: Peter Jackson
RUGGED LAND OF GOLD (NZ-Canada
    co-production)

1995
WAR STORIES Director: Gaylene Preston
CHICKEN Director: Grant Lahood
THE WHOLE OF THE MOON Director: Ian Mune
JACK BROWN GENIUS Director: Tony Hiles
BONJOUR TIMOTHY Director: Wayne Tourell
FLIGHT OF THE ALBATROSS (locations)
    Director: Werner Meyer

1996
THE CLIMB (locations) Director: Bob Swaim
BROKEN ENGLISH Director: Gregor Nicholas
THE FRIGHTENERS Director: Peter Jackson
ABERRATION Director: Tim Boxell
NIGHTMARE MAN (NZ-Canada co-production)

1997
SAVING GRACE Director: Costa Botes
TOPLESS WOMEN Talk About Their Lives
    Director: Harry Sinclair
MEMORY AND DESIRE Director: Niki Caro

THE UGLY Director: Scott Reynolds
HEAVEN Director: Scott Reynolds

1998
VIA SATELLITE Director: Anthony McCarten
I'LL MAKE YOU HAPPY Director: Athina Tsoulis
WHEN LOVE COMES Director: Garth Maxwell
THE LUNATICS' BALL Director: Michael Thorp

1999
PUNITIVE DAMAGE Director: Annie Goldson
CHANNELLING BABY Director: Christine Parker
WILD BLUE Director: Dale Bradley
THE IRREFUTABLE TRUTH ABOUT DEMONS
    Director: Glenn Standring
THE PRICE OF MILK Director: Harry Sinclair
WHAT BECOMES OF THE BROKEN HEARTED?
    Director: Ian Mune
SAVAGE HONEYMOON Director: Mark Beesley
SCARFIES Director: Robert Sarkies
HOPELESS Director: Stephen Hickey
MAGIK AND ROSE Director: Vanessa Alexander
VERTICAL LIMIT (locations)
    Director: Martin Campbell
JUBILEE Director: Michael Hurst
UNCOMFORTABLE COMFORTABLE (16mm)
    Director: Campbell Walker
FEARLESS NZ-Canada co-production

1999/2000
LORD OF THE RINGS X 3 Director: Peter Jackson

2000
THE SHIRT (digi) Director: John Laing
SHIFTER (digi) Director: Colin Hodson
THE FEATHERS OF PEACE Director: Barry Barclay
STICKMEN Director: Hamish Rothwell
SNAKESKIN Director: Gillian Ashurst
CROOKED EARTH Director: Sam Pillsbury
RAIN Director: Christine Jeffs

2001
TOY LOVE Director: Harry Sinclair
TONGAN NINJA Director: Jason Stutter
THE MAORI MERCHANT OF VENICE
    Director: Don Selwyn
HOTERE Director: Merata Mita
BLERTA Director: Geoff Murphy
HER MAJESTY (locations) Director: Mark Gordon
OFFENSIVE BEHAVIOUR (digi) Director: Patrick Gillies
HEARTS OF MEN (US telemovie) Director: Billy Graham
THE WAITING PLACE Director: Cristobal Araus Lobos

2002
NO ONE CAN HEAR YOU Director: Dale Bradley
CUPID'S PREY Director: Dale Bradley
THE VECTOR FILE Director: Eliot Christopher
EXPOSURE Director: David Blyth

MURDER IN GREENWICH (US telemovie)
    Director: Tom McLoughlin
KOMBI NATION Director: Grant Lahood
BLESSED (digi) Director: Rachel Douglas
THE WATER GIANT (locations) Director: John Henderson
IN A LAND OF PLENTY (digi) Director: Alistair Barry
WHALE RIDER Director: Niki Caro

2003
TREASURE ISLAND KIDS: The Battle of Treasure
    Island Director: Gavin Scott
TREASURE ISLAND KIDS: The Monster of Treasure
    Island Director: Michael Hurst
TREASURE ISLAND KIDS: The Mystery of Treasure
    Island Director: Michael Hurst
TERROR PEAK Director: Dale Bradley
CAVE IN Director: Rex Piano
NEMESIS GAME Director: Jesse Warn
FRACTURE Director: Larry Parr
FOR GOOD Director: Stuart McKenzie
PERFECT STRANGERS Director: Gaylene Preston
THE LOCALS Director: Greg Page
CHRISTMAS (digi) Director: Gregory King
WOODENHEAD (digi) Director: Florian Habicht
THIS IS NOT A LOVE STORY (digi)
    Director: Keith Hill
ORPHANS AND ANGELS (digi) Director: Harold Brodie
GUPTA VERSUS GUPTA (digi)
    Director: Jitendra and Promila Pal
I THINK I'M GOING (digi)
    Director: Alexander Greenhough
WHY CAN'T I STOP THIS UNCONTROLLABLE
    DANCING (digi) Director: Campbell Walker
MY GARDENER (locations) Director: Iren Koster
THE LAST SAMURAI (locations) Director: Ed Zwick
WITHOUT A PADDLE (locations)
    Director: Stephen Brill

2004
IN MY FATHER'S DEN Director: Brad McGann
SPOOKED Director: Geoff Murphy
BOOGEYMAN Director: Stephen Kay
FIFTY WAYS OF SAYING FABULOUS
    Director: Stewart Main

2005
THE WORLD'S FASTEST INDIAN
    Director: Roger Donaldson
RIVER QUEEN: Director: Vincent Ward
PERFECT CREATURE Director: Glenn Standing
THE CHRONICLES OF NARNIA – THE LION,
    THE WITCH AND THE WARDROBE
    Director: Andrew Adamson
NUMBER 2 Director: Toa Fraser
LUELLA MILLER (digi) Director: Dane Giraud
CULTIC Director: Jennifer Russell
KING KONG Director: Peter Jackson
SIONE'S WEDDING Director: Chris Graham

BEYOND REASONABLE DOUBT
1982 Cognac Festival du Film Policier
Grand Prix, John Laing

BATTLETRUCK
1982 Catalonian International Film Festival, Sitges, Spain
Clavell de Plata, Best Actress: Annie McEnroe

THE SCARECROW
1982 Mystfest
Best Artistic Contribution: Jonathan Smith,
Tracey Mann, Daniel McLaren, John Carradine,
Bruce Allpress, Philip Holder, Stephen Taylor,
Desmond Kelly, Anne Flannery, Denise O'Connell,
Jonathan Hardy

MERRY CHRISTMAS MR LAWRENCE (locations)
1984 Awards of the Japanese Academy
Most Popular Film

1984 BAFTA Awards
Best Score: Ryuichi Sakamoto

MR WRONG
1986 Mystfest
Commendation for actress Heather Bolton

THE QUIET EARTH
1986 Fantafestival
Best Actor: Bruno Lawrence
Best Direction: Geoff Murphy

THE SILENT ONE
1986 Paris Film Festival
Special Jury Prize: Yvonne Mackay
Best Actor: Telo Malase

ILLUSTRIOUS ENERGY
1988 Hawaii International Film Festival
Best Feature Film: Leon Narbey

BAD TASTE
1989 Fantafestival
Audience Award: Peter Jackson

WILLOW (Locations)
1990 Academy of Science Fiction, Fantasy and Horror Films, USA
Saturn Award for Best Costumes: Barbara Lane

FLYING FOX IN A FREEDOM TREE
1989 Tokyo International Film Festival
Best Screenplay Award: Martyn Sanderson

THE PIANO
1994 Academy Awards, USA
Oscar, Best Actress in a Leading Role: Holly Hunter
Oscar, Best Writing, Screenplay Written Directly for the Screen: Jane Campion
Oscar, Best Actress in a Supporting Role: Anna Paquin

1993 Australian Film Institute
Best Director: Jane Campion
Best Film: Jane Campion
Best Screenplay, Original: Jane Campion
Best Achievement in Cinematography: Stuart Dryburgh
Best Actress in a Lead Role: Holly Hunter
Best Achievement in Editing: Veronika Jenet
Best Actor in a Lead Role: Harvey Keitel
Best Achievement in Production Design: Andrew McAlpine
Best Original Music Score: Michael Nyman
Best Achievement in Costume Design: Janet Patterson

1994 BAFTA Film Awards
Best Actress: Holly Hunter
Best Production Design: Andrew McAlpine
Best Costume Design: Janet Patterson

1994 Bodil Awards
Best Non-American Film (Bedste ikke-amerikanske film): Jane Campion (director)

1993 Boston Society of Film Critics Awards
Best Actress: Holly Hunter

1993 Camerimage
Golden Frog: Stuart Dryburgh

1993 Cannes Film Festival
Palme d'Or: Jane Campion
Best Actress: Holly Hunter (tied with Ba wang bie ji)

1994 Chicago Film Critics Association Awards
Best Foreign Language Film
Best Actress: Holly Hunter
Best Score: Michael Nyman

1994 César Awards, France
Best Foreign Film (Meilleur film étranger): Jane Campion

1994 Dallas-Fort Worth Film Critics Association Awards
Best Actress: Holly Hunter

1994 Golden Globes, USA
Best Performance by an Actress in a Motion Picture — Drama: Holly Hunter
Best Motion Picture — Drama

1994 Guldbagge Awards
Best Foreign Film (Bästa utländska film)

1994 Independent Spirit Awards
Best Foreign Film: Jane Campion

1995 Kinema Junpo Awards
Best Foreign Language Film: Jane Campion

1994 London Critics Circle Film Awards
Film of the Year
Actress of the Year: Holly Hunter

1993 Los Angeles Film Critics Association Awards
Best Director: Jane Campion
Best Screenplay: Jane Campion
Best Cinematography: Stuart Dryburgh (tied with Janusz Kaminski for *Schindler's List*)
Best Actress: Holly Hunter
Best Supporting Actor: Anna Paquin (tied with Rosie Perez in *Fearless*.)

1994 Motion Picture Sound Editors, USA
Best Sound Editing — Foreign Feature

1993 National Board of Review, USA
Best Actress: Holly Hunter

1994 National Society of Film Critics Awards, USA
Best Screenplay: Jane Campion
Best Actress: Holly Hunter

1993 New York Film Critics Circle Awards
Best Director: Jane Campion
Best Screenplay: Jane Campion
Best Actress: Holly Hunter

1994 PGA Golden Laurel Awards
Nova Award
Most Promising Producer in Theatrical Motion Pictures: Jan Chapman

1994 Robert Festival
Best Foreign Film (Årets udenlandske spillefilm): Jane Campion (director)

1994 Southeastern Film Critics Association Awards
Best Picture
Best Director: Jane Campion
Best Actress: Holly Hunter

1993 Vancouver International Film Festival
Most Popular Film

1994 Writers Guild of America, USA
Best Screenplay Written Directly for the Screen: Jane Campion

BRAINDEAD
1994 Academy of Science Fiction, Fantasy and Horror Films, USA
Saturn Award

1993 Amsterdam Fantastic Film Festival
Silver Scream Award: Peter Jackson

1993 Avoriaz Fantastic Film Festival
Grand Prize: Peter Jackson

1992 Catalonian International Film Festival, Sitges, Spain
Best Special Effects: Richard Taylor, Bob McCarron

1992 Fantafestival
Best Actor: Timothy Balme
Best Special Effects

1993 Fantasporto
International Fantasy Film Award Best Special Effects:
Steve Ingram
International Fantasy Film Award Best Film:
Peter Jackson

ONCE WERE WARRIORS
1995 Australian Film Institute
Best Foreign Film Award: Robin Scholes

1995 Fantasporto
Best Actress: Rena Owen
Critics' Award — Special Mention
Best Film: Lee Tamahori

1994 Montréal World Film Festival
Best Actress: Rena Owen
(tied with Helena Bergström in *Sista dansen*)
Grand Prix des Amériques: Lee Tamahori
Prize of the Ecumenical Jury: Lee Tamahori
Public Prize: Lee Tamahori

1995 Rotterdam International Film Festival
Audience Award: Lee Tamahori

1994 San Diego International Film Festival
Best Actress: Rena Owen

1994 Venice Film Festival
Anicaflash Prize: Lee Tamahori

HEAVENLY CREATURES
1996 Empire Awards, UK
Best British Actress: Kate Winslet

1995 Gérardmer Film Festival
Grand Prize: Peter Jackson

1996 London Critics Circle Film Awards
Director of the Year: Peter Jackson
British Actress of the Year: Kate Winslet

1994 Toronto International Film Festival
Metro Media Award: Peter Jackson

1994 Venice Film Festival
Silver Lion: Peter Jackson

THE WHOLE OF THE MOON
1996 Giffoni Film Festival
Bronze Gryphon for Best Actor: Toby Fisher
Golden Gryphon: Ian Mune
Bronze Gryphon for Best Actress: Nikki Si'Ulepa

BONJOUR TIMOTHY
1996 Berlin International Film Festival
Honorable Mention: Wayne Tourell

THE CLIMB (locations)
1998 Berlin International Film Festival
UNICEF Award: Bob Swaim

1999 Temecula Valley International Film Festival
Viewer's Choice Award for Best Feature Film:
Bob Swaim

THE FRIGHTENERS
1996 Catalonian International Film Festival, Sitges, Spain
Best Special Effects: Richard Taylor

TOPLESS WOMEN Talk About Their Lives
1998 Fantasporto
Audience Jury Award: Harry Sinclair

1997 Thessaloniki Film Festival
Special Mention: Harry Sinclair

THE UGLY
1997 Catalonian International Film Festival, Sitges, Spain
Best Director: Scott Reynolds

1997 Fantafestiva;
Best Actor: Paolo Rotondo

1998 Fantasporto
International Fantasy Film Award for Best Actress:
Rebecca Hobbs
Special Mention: Scott Reynolds, for an outstanding
first feature.

1997 Puchon International Fantastic Film Festival
Citizen's Choice Award: Scott Reynolds

HEAVEN
1999 Fant-Asia Film Festival
Best International Film: Scott Reynolds

THE LUNATICS' BALL
1999 Shanghai International Film Festival
Special Jury Award: Michael Thorp

PUNITIVE DAMAGE
2000 Cinemanila International Film Festival
Best Documentary: Annie Goldson

1999 Munich Film Festival
MediaNet Award in Silver: Annie Goldson

2000 San Francisco International Film Festival
Certificate of Merit for Film & Video — Current
Event: Annie Goldson

THE PRICE OF MILK
2001 Fantasporto
Critics' Award: Harry Sinclair
Nominated, International Fantasy Film Award Best
Film: Harry Sinclair

2001 Puchon International Fantastic Film Festival
Best of Puchon: Harry Sinclair

MAGIK AND ROSE
2001 Fantasporto
Directors' Week Award — Special Mention:
Vanessa Alexander

VERTICAL LIMIT (locations)
2001 Golden Trailer Awards
Best Action(tied with *Gone in Sixty Seconds*)

LORD OF THE RINGS — FoTR
(As the total awards and nominations for all three of the Rings trilogy are too numerous to mention in detail, only major awards are noted in these pages)

2002 AFI Awards, USA
Production Designer of the Year: Grant Major
Movie of the Year: Barrie M. Osborne, Peter Jackson,
Fran Walsh, Tim Sanders
Digital Effects Artist of the Year: Jim Rygiel

2002 ASCAP Film and Television Music Awards
Top Box Office Films: Howard Shore

2002 Academy Awards, USA
Oscar, Best Cinematography: Andrew Lesnie
Oscar, Best Makeup: Peter Owen, Richard Taylor
Oscar, Best Effects, Visual Effects: Jim Rygiel,
Randall William Cook, Richard Taylor,
Mark Stetson
Oscar, Best Music, Original Score: Howard Shore

2003 Academy of Science Fiction, Fantasy and Horror Films, USA
Saturn Award, Best Fantasy Film
Saturn Award, Best Director: Peter Jackson

2002 BAFTA Awards
Audience Award
Best Film: Peter Jackson, Barrie M. Osborne,
Tim Sanders
David Lean Award for Direction: Peter Jackson
Best Make Up/Hair: Peter Owen, Peter King,
Richard Taylor
Best Achievement in Special Visual Effects: Jim Rygiel,
Richard Taylor, Alex Funke, Randall William Cook,
Mark Stetson
Best Editing: John Gilbert

2002 MTV Movie Awards
Best Movie
Breakthrough Male Performance: Orlando Bloom

2003 People's Choice Awards, USA
Favorite Dramatic Motion Picture
Favorite Motion Picture

LORD OF THE RINGS — TTT
2003 Academy Awards, USA
Oscar for Best Visual Effects: Jim Rygiel, Joe Letteri,
Randall William Cook, Alex Funke
Oscar for Best Sound Editing: Ethan Van der Ryn,
Mike Hopkins

2003 Australian Film Institute
Best Foreign Film Award: Peter Jackson,
Barrie M. Osborne, Fran Walsh

2003 BAFTA Awards
Audience Award
Best Costume Design: Ngila Dickson, Richard Taylor
Best Achievement in Special Visual Effects: Jim Rygiel,
Joe Letteri, Randall William Cook, Alex Funke

2004 Grammy Awards
Best Score Soundtrack Album for a Motion Picture,
Television or Other Visual Media: Howard Shore

2003 MTV Movie Awards
Best Action Sequence: The battle for Helms Deep
Best Movie
Best Virtual Performance: For 'Gollum'
Best On-Screen Team: Elijah Wood, Sean Astin,
'Gollum'

2004 People's Choice Awards, USA
Favorite Dramatic Motion Picture

LORD OF THE RINGS — ROTK
2004 Academy Awards, USA
Oscar for Best Sound: Christopher Boyes, Michael
Semanick, Michael Hedges, Hammond Peek
Oscar for Best Costume Design: Ngila Dickson,
Richard Taylor
Oscar for Best Director: Peter Jackson

Oscar for Best Art Direction-Set Decoration:
Grant Major (art director), Dan Hennah (set
decorator), Alan Lee (set decorator)
Oscar for Best Picture: Barrie M. Osborne,
Peter Jackson, Fran Walsh
Oscar for Best Visual Effects: Jim Rygiel, Joe Letteri,
Randall William Cook, Alex Funke
Oscar for Best Editing: Jamie Selkirk
Oscar for Best Music, Original Score: Howard Shore
Oscar for Best Makeup: Richard Taylor, Peter King
Oscar for Best Writing, Screenplay Based on Material
Previously Produced or Published: Fran Walsh,
Philippa Boyens, Peter Jackson
Oscar for Best Music, Original Song: Fran Walsh,
Howard Shore, Annie Lennox for the song 'Into
the West'

2004 Australian Film Institute
Best Foreign Film: Peter Jackson, Barrie M. Osborne,
Fran Walsh

2004 BAFTA Awards
Audience Award
Best Achievement in Special Visual Effects: Joe Letteri,
Jim Rygiel, Randall William Cook, Alex Funke
Best Film: Barrie M. Osborne, Fran Walsh, Peter
Jackson
Best Cinematography: Andrew Lesnie
Best Screenplay — Adapted: Fran Walsh, Philippa
Boyens, Peter Jackson

2004 Golden Globes, USA
Best Motion Picture — Drama
Best Director — Motion Picture: Peter Jackson
Best Original Score — Motion Picture: Howard Shore
Best Original Song — Motion Picture: Howard Shore,
Fran Walsh, Annie Lennox for the song 'Into the
West'.

2005 Grammy Awards
Best Song Written for a Motion Picture, Television or
Other Visual Media: Annie Lennox, Howard Shore,
Fran Walsh for the song 'Into The West'.
Best Score Soundtrack Album for a Motion Picture,
Television or Other Visual Media: Howard Shore

2004 MTV Movie Awards
Best Action Sequence: The battle at Gondor
Best Movie

THE MAORI MERCHANT OF VENICE
2002 Hawaii International Film Festival
Audience Award
Best Feature: Don Selwyn

HER MAJESTY (locations)
2002 Chicago International Children's Film Festival
Children's Jury Award
North American Feature Film or Video — Live-Action:
Mark J. Gordon

2004 Florida Film Festival
Audience Award
Best International Feature: Mark J. Gordon

2002 Heartland Film Festival
Truly Moving Sound Award
Crystal Heart Award: Mark J. Gordon

2002 Marco Island Film Festival
Rising Star Award: Sally Andrews
Audience Award
Best International Feature: Mark J. Gordon
Best Narrative Feature: Mark J. Gordon
Dale Meriborne Herlotz Award for Excellence in Music:
William Ross

2004 Newport Beach Film Festival
Audience Award
Best Independent Feature: Mark J. Gordon

2004 Ojai Film Festival
Best Narrative Feature: Mark J. Gordon

2004 Palm Beach International Film Festival
Special Jury Prize: Sally Andrews for a feature film
début performance.

2004 San Diego Film Festival
Best Actress: Sally Andrews

2004 Stony Brook Film Festival
Audience Choice Award
Best Feature: Mark J. Gordon

WHALE RIDER
2003 BAFTA Awards
Children's Award
Best Feature Film: Tim Sanders, John Barnett,
Frank Hübner, Niki Caro

2004 Broadcast Film Critics Association Awards
Best Young Actor/Actress: Keisha Castle-Hughes

2004 Chicago Film Critics Association Awards
Most Promising Performer: Keisha Castle-Hughes

2003 Chicago International Children's Film Festival
Children's Jury Award
Live-Action Feature Film or Video: Niki Caro

2004 Cinemanila International Film Festival
Special Jury Prize: Niki Caro

2003 Environmental Media Awards, USA
Feature Film

2003 Humanitas Prize
Sundance Film Category: Niki Caro

2004 Image Awards

2004 Independent Spirit Awards
Best Foreign Film: Niki Caro

2004 Mexico City International Contemporary Film Festival
Special Award
Best Humanitarian Content: Niki Caro

2004 Online Film Critics Society Awards
Best Breakthrough Performance: Keisha Castle-Hughes

2003 Rotterdam International Film Festival
Audience Award: Niki Caro

2003 San Francisco International Film Festival Audience Award
Best Narrative Feature: Niki Caro
(tied with *The Cuckoo*)

2003 Seattle International Film Festival
Golden Space Needle Award for Best Film
Golden Space Needle Award for Best Director:
Niki Caro

2003 Sundance Film Festival
Audience Award, World Cinema: Niki Caro

2003 São Paulo International Film Festival
International Jury Award: Niki Caro

2004 Toronto International Film Festival
People's Choice Award: Niki Caro

2004 Young Artist Awards
Best International Feature Film
Best Young Actress in an International Film:
Keisha Castle-Hughes

PERFECT STRANGERS
2004 Fantasporto
Directors' Week Award for Best Actress: Rachael Blake

THIS IS NOT A LOVE STORY (digi)
2002 Dances With Films
Best Screenplay: Keith Hill

THE LAST SAMURAI (locations)
2004 ASCAP Film and Television Music Awards
Top Box Office Films: Hans Zimmer

IN MY FATHER'S DEN
2005 British Independent Film Awards
Most Promising Newcomer: Emily Barclay

2005 Dinard British Film Festival
Kodak Award for Best Cinematography:
Stuart Dryburgh
Audience Award: Brad McGann
Golden Hitchcock: Brad McGann

2004 San Sebastián International Film Festival
Youth Jury Award: Brad McGann

2005 Seattle International Film Festival
New Director's Showcase Special Jury Prize:
Brad McGann

2005 Stony Brook Film Festival
Best Feature: Brad McGann
(tied with *Ellis in Glamourland*)

2004 Toronto International Film Festival
International Critics' Award (FIPRESCI):
Brad McGann

THE CHRONICLES OF NARNIA — THE LION, THE WITCH and THE WARDROBE
2006 Academy Awards, USA
Oscar for Best Achievement in Makeup:
Howard Berger, Tami Lane

2006 BAFTA Awards
Best Make Up/Hair: Howard Berger, Gregory Nicotero, Nikki Gooley
Best Achievement in Special Visual Effects: Dean
Wright, Bill Westenhofer, Jim Berney, Scott Farrar

2006 Broadcast Film Critics Association Awards
Best Family Film (Live Action)

2006 Motion Picture Sound Editors, USA
Best Breakthrough Performance: Georgie Henley

Satellite Awards 2005
Outstanding Motion Picture, Animated or Mixed Media

KING KONG
2006 Academy Awards, USA
Oscar for Best Achievement in Sound: Christopher Boyes, Michael Semanick, Michael Hedges, Hammond Peek
Oscar for Best Achievement in Sound Editing:
Mike Hopkins, Ethan Van der Ryn
Oscar for Best Achievement in Visual Effects:
Joe Letteri, Brian Van't Hul, Christian Rivers, Richard Taylor
Oscar for Best Achievement in Art Direction:
Grant Major

2006 BAFTA Awards
Best Achievement in Special Visual Effects: Joe Letteri, Christian Rivers, Brian Van't Hul, Richard Taylor, Peter Jackson

Index